Football Fundamentals
for Kids and Parents

Football Fundamentals for Kids and Parents

Jerry W. Betts

Foreword by Paul W. "Bear" Bryant

South Brunswick and New York: A. S. Barnes and Company

London: Thomas Yoseloff Ltd

A. S. Barnes and Co., Inc.
Cranbury, New Jersey 08512

Thomas Yoseloff Ltd
Magdalen House
136-148 Tooley Street
London SE1 2TT, England

Library of Congress Cataloging in Publication Data

Betts, Jerry W   , 1936-
    Football fundamentals for kids and parents.

    Includes index.
    SUMMARY: An introduction to the fundamentals of football for coaches,
beginning players, and parents.
    1. Football coaching—Juvenile literature.
[1. Football]   I. Title.
GV956.6.B37 1978   796.33'2077   77-84561
    (cloth) ISBN 0-498-02067-3
    (paper) ISBN 0-498-02304-4

The diagrams for this book have been expertly prepared by Marilyn Franklin.

Printed in the United States of America

Contents

Foreword

Growing up on a small farm in Moro Bottom, Arkansas, didn't provide a lot of so-called advantages for a youngster. The only instruction I can remember getting before I played a football game was to try to kill anyone on the other team. The only equipment I had—and this came later—was putting some cleats on the only pair of shoes I had. Football for me as a youngster was not much more than a substitute for fighting.

Football has been good to me for over forty years. It gave me a chance I would never have had otherwise, and I think I've learned a lot about people and living through football.

I can't say that football would have been any better for me with proper instruction and equipment, but there's no question that it's next to essential today.

As in most everything, the fundamentals of football today are the same as they were when Coach Frank Thomas and Coach Hank Crisp were teaching them to me when I came to the University of Alabama in 1931, and they'll be the same fifty years from now. Which is not to say that football hasn't changed, because it has. But you still start with the basics.

I was intrigued by the title of this book, and I feel that it has an important place in football. Certainly I was never encouraged to play football; neither of my parents ever saw a football game in their lives. But parents have an important role to play if their children are going to play football. This book can help them as well as their children.

Football is a way of life for me. It's not going to be that way for everyone. But it can help you learn values that will be an important part of your life regardless of what you do. Whatever you do, you should try to do it as well as you can. If you do that in football there's a better chance that you will try to do it in everything else, and you'll be a better person for it.

Paul W. "Bear" Bryant
Head Football Coach
University of Alabama

Introduction

Little league baseball was born back in 1939 and has been an accepted part of the American scene for over three decades, but football for athletes of grade school age is relatively new and considerably more controversial. *Life* magazine published an article several years ago* that pointed out some of its potentially serious drawbacks, emphasizing not only the development of "win at all cost" pressures but the possibly hazardous effects of injuries on children whose bones are not yet fully formed. More recent criticism has been leveled, and psychologists have been joined by high school and college coaches who claim that poor coaching in junior leagues teaches mistakes that are sometimes difficult to unlearn in later development.

However much truth there may be in the attacks of the detractors, it looks like youth football is here to stay, and if you do not believe it look around your neighborhood some September afternoon after school. Not only in terms of numbers of kids participating or numbers of parents and friends observing, but in terms of dollars spent on equipment

*November 15, 1963.

and support, youth league football is a going concern. In fact, many a youngster who aspires to play football in high school and college these days is afraid that if he does not begin in the youth leagues he may be giving up an experience edge he may have trouble regaining. If that does not bother junior, it often bothers Dad.

My purpose is not to argue the merits of whether kids should or should not get into football when they are nine and ten years old, but to outline some principles that should be followed by those who do. They will learn habits in those early years, and those habits are likely to stay with them, good or bad. And many parents, including those who are pressed into coaching service, know little more about the game than the thirty or so raw youngsters who stand there facing them on that first day of practice. What they know, both parent and aspiring player, is a confusing array of football spectacular ranging from Alabama's crunching wishbone offense to Miami's devastating variations from the pro set.

So what's wrong with college and professional football? Nothing! In fact, they are beautiful to watch. But they are the products of individual and team development built on as many as ten years of experience for the average college ball player.

To insure that the young potential grid hero gets his experience the right way, parents, whether they are coaching or not, should know the fundamentals of football and how they should be taught. They should also be interested enough in their children to make sure that they are being taught correctly. This book is not an advanced text but a grade school primer on football for youth leaguers and their parents.

Football Fundamentals for Kids and Parents

Part I

Getting Started

1
The Coach and the League

Football is a violent game. It is also an emotional game, played to win. In dealing with young people who are getting their first formal exposure to the game, coaches and the leagues in which they usually divide themselves must agree on some basic ground rules from the very outset. That appears to be a logical place to begin a book on youth league fundamentals.

The first stumbling block to playing organized football is usually Mama. Many mothers do not like their sons playing football because they are afraid of injuries. And that is not wrong. But we can influence that opinion, and the first thing any football organization must think about is insuring that all reasonable measures are taken to keep injuries to an absolute minimum.

Equipment is the first consideration. Never scrimp on equipment. If there are insufficient funds to buy complete uniforms, do not play. A complete uniform should consist of helmet with face guard, athletic supporter (preferably with

The proper equipment for a youth leaguer.

plastic cup), shoulder pads, pants with thigh and knee pads, kidney pads, mouthpiece, shoes (with soccer type or short cleats), sweat socks, and jersey or sweat shirt.

Once that has been taken care of, almost as important is the conduct of the game itself. Most youth football leagues play by high school or junior high school rules, and games should never be played without at least two adult referees who are familiar with the rule book. In fact, copies of the rule book should be made available to everybody associated with the league as mandatory reading. However, there are some aspects of the game, due to the experience they require, that tend to result in more injuries than others, and many leagues make additional rules eliminating kickoffs, blitzing, and other specifics and limiting the number and duration of practices and restricting the number of formations that can be used.

Agreements concerning these and any other plays that parents and coaches feel should be deleted or controlled based on the level of experience of the players must be made in the very beginning. Kickoffs and blitzing, for example, require special practice and deviate somewhat from pure, first-step, fundamental football. Kickoffs, in particular, seem hard for beginners to handle and are better avoided until players have gained ability in downfield blocking and tackling. It is often easier to make a league rule eliminating them for players up to twelve years old, spotting the ball instead on the receiving team's thirty-five-yard line. Blitzing, also called red-dogging (planned rushing from the defensive backfield) is harder to control but is sometimes ruled out because of the element of surprise it creates. Restricting it doesn't keep a defensive back from reading a play, rushing across the line of scrimmage and making the tackle in the offensive backfield, but it prevents the defensive back from making a premeditated rush, something that can play havoc with beginners' blocking assignments. If anyone is worried that in leaving out elements of play the kids will be shortchanged, that is not so. At least in the beginning they will be having enough trouble handling straight-ahead blocking and tackling. There will be plenty of time later to add complexity, and the less they have to learn the better they will learn it. Football is a game of reading keys and reacting, and the simpler the environment at the start, the easier it will be for them to learn to read and react.

Coaching philosophy is another concern for early thought. Grantland Rice said, "Its not that you won or lost but how you played the game," and modern-day big-time cynics have been ridiculing the words ever since. Anyone remotely familiar with football knows the tremendous competitiveness it generates—competitiveness that often surfaces in aggressiveness. It is particularly evident in the very physical arena of the "pit," that narrow strip between the offensive and defensive linemen so difficult for referees to observe. Inevitably the resulting play becomes very rough, and some players develop techniques that include deliberate gouging, tripping, elbowing, and holding, which are all against the rules. The kids have heard about it, too, and some will ask to be taught how to do it. Do you teach and condone survival football?

A youngster at this age is very impressionable, and he is searching for the values that he will carry through life. A book on fundamental football may seem a strange place for moralizing, but the athletic field is too fine a training ground for young men to learn honesty and fair play to ignore. Teaching or condoning tactics that deliberately violate the rules is totally inconsistent with what should be the goals of youth league football. There is enough hypocrisy to go around without introducing it on the football field.

In a more practical vein, the ten-year-old football player should have his hands full just learning to make an effective block or tackle without trying to add the underhanded variations that are difficult in themselves if they are to go undetected. Anyway, when he gets caught it will cost the team fifteen yards when they can least afford it. He will have plenty of time after he has mastered the fundamentals to learn to defend himself, and at this stage the best protection is good execution. There is no place in youth football for deliberate dirty play.

Winning is another favorite subject, and winning, of course, is what football is all about. Everybody wants his team to win, and anyone who has not read about little league winning in Max Schulman's *Rally Round the Flag Boys* should. But too much has been written about the dehumanizing affects of "win at all cost" football to not make mention of it here. No child should ever be taught that it does not matter whether he wins or loses. But neither should he be taught that in winning anything is justified. The tough question confronting coach and parent is—where do you draw the line between the learning and the winning? And there is no easy answer.

This concern becomes particularly difficult when the coach is trying to give all of his players a chance to play against a better, more experienced team, and every time he replaces his first team the opponents run all over his weaker substitutes. Some leagues make provision for this by requiring each player to spend a *minimum of time in each game or playing reserves during the second and fourth quarters*. All leagues should have and enforce such a rule. It is not easy. The bookkeeping is demanding and momentum is lost when teams change over, discouraging starters and their parents, and teams are required to have equal or almost equal numbers of players. Obviously, twenty-two man teams are very desirable. But who plays and how much is never an easy question, and it is a question that each league and each coach must consider very carefully. It is also something the parents must understand. And the words *careful consideration* sum up the basic responsibility, accepted by every coach and every parent of youth league football players.

The use of *parent and coach* as a team in early-development football is deliberate and significant. The people who volunteer to go out on the field with these little guys to teach them how to play join the ranks of the teachers, Sunday school teachers, and den mothers of the community. Their positions of influence make them teacher, advisor, and builder of youthful character to your children. The parent who does not volunteer but also does not provide support is delegating a very heavy responsibility. This does not mean that coaching, even of little leaguers, can be a committee endeavor: it absolutely cannot. The coach must be the undisputed boss on the field, and parents should stay away from players during the game. They should not even be permitted near the players' bench. They belong in the stands. But when the coaches lack experience, as is so often the case, interested parents should know enough and care enough to want to provide guidance and assistance to keep things on track.

So whether you are on the field coaching or on the sidelines cheering the kids on, you have a responsibility. These young people are learning football, but they are also learning values that are likely to stay with them for the rest of their lives. Parents who are indifferent or who try to influence events to satisfy their own selfish ambitions must do so with the full knowledge of the negative effects it will have on the kids and on the value of youth league football.

2
Conditioning

If we think about it at all, we think of our children as being infinitely elastic, full of energy, and capable of running and playing virtually without limits. It is not so. Even nine- and ten-year-olds need a period of conditioning to prepare them to play football. In fact, for a number of different reasons, a well-planned, deliberate period of conditioning is one of the most important steps a young first-year ball player can undergo in learning the game.

Football requires the use of muscles in a physically and emotionally demanding competitive environment, and the only way to insure proper preparation is to condition them under similar conditions. Even the neighborhood spark plug who never seems to wear down must work up gradually to the physical violence and dynamic strain of football. Remember, when he's home running around the yard he rests when he needs to. On the playing field he often has to draw on reserve energy when he would rather be sitting down resting. But there are benefits of the conditioning period beyond toning the muscles.

Conditioning can be effectively used to teach the immature athlete the physical and mental discipline of preparing for athletics. Any mature athlete will tell you that you just do not rush into competition unprepared. But nine-year-olds do not know that, and there is no better way to teach them than in the preseason grind. Before any season and before any game the trained athlete goes through a warm-up drill designed to loosen and stretch his muscles and prepare him emotionally for the competition ahead. Too many high school athletes today have never learned this important lesson.

Discipline is even more important. Athletics demand a great deal of discipline, and this is something for which many young ballplayers are ill prepared. Success in football is built around a group of athletes working together physically and emotionally to achieve a common goal. Watch the kids at play sometime and it will be quickly obvious that teamwork is not the natural condition of the neighborhood. It has to be learned, and to be learned it has to be taught from the first day.

A well-prepared coaching staff has a carefully developed routine that they introduce at the first practice session. Practices are limited, and there is never time to do everything that should be done, particularly if they are restricted to two or three a week, which is most often the case with athletes at this age, often because of limited coaching availability. If an effective team is to be developed it takes planning and control to make the most efficient use of the time. As the season wears on, practice sessions will become complicated by the necessity to concentrate on specialties, often resulting in dividing the team into smaller groups. Only during the initial conditioning period does the coach have the luxury of working with the entire team under nonstress conditions. That period should be used to establish discipline and create the necessary coach-team relationship.

The properly disciplined team will make it a point to be punctual for practice, starting warm-up drills on their own to be ready to practice when the coach arrives. This can save a lot of practice time because, unlike full-time coaches, the volunteer coach is usually coming from his regular job. Such a team will also develop team character more quickly. Only the quarterback talks in the huddle; only the designated captain talks to the referee; and the team listens when the coach is talking. These are little things that go toward making a football team yet do not come naturally to young players. If the kids do not learn them early they will come much harder later on.

A good conditioning period also provides a chance for the coaches to see what they have. It will not take long to determine which boys really want to play ball, which ones are strong and coordinated, and which ones are the natural leaders. The leaders become particularly important with inexperienced players since the coach cannot be on the field during a game to maintain order and confidence. From the very first practice a concerted effort must be made to establish leadership from among the ranks of the players themselves. It will make the difference when the going gets tough. To get it started, once the routine has been established, the boys should be encouraged to conduct the exercises during the preliminary warm-up period with the coaches backing them up to make sure they get the cooperation they need from the rest of the team and counseling them when they become overbearing. And they can become overbearing if permitted to do so.

Early practices will set the tempo for the remainder of the season. If the normal initial confusion is allowed to endure, difficulty will be experienced in getting rid of it as the season progresses. Nine- and ten-year-olds often find it hard to settle down under the best of circumstances. Coaches should not hesitate to start right out with standard punishments:

laps around the field, windsprints, and push-ups. But they should be careful to be fair, impartial, unemotional, and to never humiliate. And parents must understand and lend them support.

The conditioning period should begin with a three-week program provided for the players prior to the beginning of formal practice so they can begin getting ready on their own. It should consist of specified and increasing series of walking, jogging, and stretching exercises. Next follows several weeks of light practice, without contact, concentrating on calisthenics, running, such fundamentals as the three-point stance and signal drill, and drills consisting of stretching, isometrics, sprints, and running backward for agility. Another good exercise is the grass drill, where players, from running in place, flop on their stomachs and flip over on their backs on signal, then jump back up to running in place. This is particularly effective in teaching the body to absorb shock when it hits the ground but is also a good conditioner.

Sounds easy enough, doesn't it? But after "fooling around" all summer it comes as a shocker to the kids. Parents should be prepared for their sons to come home feeling and acting like they are exhausted, complaining about how impossible it all is. Do not give in or let them give in to themselves. If the first weeks are not tough they will not be in condition when the season starts. And that is when they run the risk of real injury. It goes without saying, however, that common sense is required on everybody's part. Early practice must be geared to the condition of the players, and although the team members must be pushed to extend themselves, it cannot be overdone. But parents who listen to the kids tell it will think coaches are murdering them with only five minutes of grass drills. Encourage them, give them plenty of water to drink and lots of salt on their food, but do not let them start feeling sorry for themselves.

During the second week helmets and perhaps shoulder pads are usually added, more to familiarize the boys with the encumbrance than to provide protection. During this period they should be taught the basic offensive and defensive formations and receive their first exposure to pass patterns and "play book" drill, learning play assignments while continuing to concentrate on conditioning.

One thing that should always be kept in mind—the players are only nine and ten years old and many have no initial training in football fundamentals. Coaches should assume nothing, but should not belabor either. At that age kids learn quickly but have a short attention span and learn better by doing. They are also quick to believe that they know it all and have nothing else to learn, a fact that adds to a coach's challenge. It's not uncommon to hear, "Why do we have to do that again? We already know how to do that." This is a challenge to the coach's practice system. Innovative practice sessions go a long way toward holding their interest. Activities should be mixed up. Making contests of the drills, particularly during the conditioning period, is helpful. Relays are good, as are races and other "games" that capture their imagination and competitive spirit. They should be given a good workout, yet drudgery should be avoided wherever possible.

As the season progresses the games may not occupy such a prevalent position in the practices, but the diversion in the drills is as important as ever. A series of drills with essentially the same purpose will have better results than a single drill that soon becomes boring to them. Even while recognizing the importance of teaching the serious nature and the discipline of the game, the coaching staff should strive to make it fun. It does not take much effort to make practice enjoyable without sacrificing productivity. The coach's attitude and his enthusiasm will be an important factor. And the parents' support and interest can influence both the coach and the players if that interest is directed toward the good of the team and not the glorification of individual players.

3
The Three-Point Stance

In any discussion of fundamentals one significant rule must be observed: keep it simple. In this day of highly sophisticated and rapidly changing offensive and defensive formations, success still depends on good fundamentals, but that is easy to forget when you are being swept up in the glamour of the sophistication. The first thing a coach should teach beginning football players is the basic position they must assume on the line of scrimmage, the three-point stance.

But everybody knows how to get into a three-point stance. Besides, each individual has his own style and should work out what is most comfortable for himself, sort of doing his own thing. Don't you believe it! The three-point stance, or the "down" position, is not natural and it is not comfortable. It must be taught, and there is a right way to teach it. If the player wants to adjust himself later to his strengths, weaknesses, and personal physical makeup, that's fine. But he must first learn the correct basic position and understand what it can do for him. Once it is learned, everything should be done from a three-point stance. It must become so familiar that it is assumed without any conscious effort—correctly. During the conditioning period it should be emphasized in everything that is done. The kids should run sprints and relays from it. They should roll from it, sommersault from it, bear-walk from it, duck-walk from it, and of course, run plays and block from it.

Before going into a detailed discussion of the three-point stance, it might be well to review some of the arguments the kids offer concerning it. They run something like, "I'm a back and Larry Czonka never gets down like that." Or, "Fred Biletnikoff doesn't line up like that and I want to be a wide receiver like him." It should be clear to anyone who knows kids that they will tell you how it ought to be because they have watched television and they KNOW how it ought to be, and it is just like their particular hero does it. Whoever tries to tell them anything different had better be prepared for an argument. In the case of the three-point stance every boy should learn it regardless of the position he is going to play because it is the first step in learning about balance, momentum, and follow through. Other positions can be covered when the time comes, but as variations of the basic position and not something entirely new. Fundamentals first. And keep it as simple as possible.

To start the boys, place their feet parellel, with the toes of the rear foot (usually the right) about even with the instep of the front foot. This may be varied later for comfort and balance by moving one foot up or back, but not too much. Now they should flex their knees, crouching slightly. This is often referred to as the boxer's stance and is basic in many sports as a position of balance. Next, bend their knees and place their forearms on them. This is the ready position. Finally, for the set position, they should place the hand opposite the lead foot on the ground about eighteen inches in front of the trailing foot, knuckles down, so that about a third of their weight rests on the hand and two-thirds is supported

The correct three-point stance

on the balls of the feet. The back should be parallel to the ground with the eyes focusing on a point about a yard in front of them or through the feet of the defensive linemen opposing them.

If this sounds trivial, remember that the position is not only unfamiliar but cramped and uncomfortable to the average schoolboy, and it must become second nature to him before the season begins. And they should not be discouraged. It takes a while for some kids to get the hang of it; in fact, there are children who never do master the three-point stance, although few continue in football beyond the youth league level.

The points to stress are balance, not too much weight on

the hand; back parallel to the ground with the bends of the legs at nearly right (90°) angles; and eyes looking at a point about a yard in front of them. There is a first tendency to want to look straight down at the ground, and next they will want to look directly at the man they intend to block. Looking straight down they see nothing, and looking at the opponent tips their intentions. They should do neither.

Now they are ready to run from this position. They should get down in cadence; READY: feet placed, knees flexed, forearms on the knees, SET: assume the down position; followed by the signals hut-one, hut-two, hut-three; running ten yards, stopping on a whistle. Then they line up and do it all over again. The hated ten-yard wind sprint on two. But always from the three-point stance and always in cadence with someone calling signals! They have to get used to signals, and that is another thing totally new to beginners. Offsides and motion penalties will be among the young team's biggest headaches.

One popular variation is the four-point stance, favored by many defensive linemen but also used sometimes on offense, particularly by the fullback in the wishbone offense. It is exactly the same except that the other hand, knuckles down, is also placed on the ground about even with its mate, directly in front of the lead foot. Often the stance is elongated somewhat with the hands farther forward, or the body more extended, than in the three-point stance, placing more weight forward and improving straight ahead drive although cutting down on balance and flexibility.

Before leaving the stance, something should be said about driving out of the down position. On the snap signal the players should be continually reminded that they know the signal on offense and this gives them an advantage that must be exploited by getting the jump on the defense. They should step out with the back foot, driving out in a sprinting stride, keeping the feet spread to achieve maximum balance and the head up to read the keys and track the opponent. Feet are an

The correct four-point stance

important consideration for beginners, who sometimes have a tendency to put one in front of the other or cross one over the other, resulting in getting "tangled up." They become critical when a blocker or tackler has to move laterally. The spread of the feet then provides a stable base that must be practiced during heavy diets of drill. But caution them— never, ever cross one foot over the other.

Again you may get arguments. Maybe Joe Green does it a little differently, or Barney Chavous's style differs as well. But fundamentals first. When the kids have the basics down pat, then they can experiment. Everybody should learn it the same way first—the right way—and they should understand what it does for them. The basic down position provides them with a balanced starting position from which it is difficult to be knocked over. If you push on their shoulders and knock their hand away to show them how stable they are it will reinforce what you are telling them. Yet they can drive quickly forward, right, left, or even backward. And *that's* what football is all about.

The universality of this position is such that parents can help their players during the preseason or on off-days if they are having trouble. Extra help and individual attention at this stage in their development can speed up the learning process, avert mistakes, and increase their confidence so that they will be ready for blocking and tackling. Often coaches are not able to spend the time they should with kids having trouble. Unlike new math and chemistry, the three-point stance is straightforward and easy to teach. But there is a right way. If the boys could see themselves, they would not need someone to teach them, but they can not. So parents can provide valuable assistance. It also shows that you care.

One tip for parents. A camera can do wonders in helping a child to learn what his mistakes are. Take a couple of pictures of him from various angles and let him compare them to the correct stance. Finally, if a parent has only a little time to spend in helping to coach the team it is most valuably spent in the first two or three weeks. That is the time when individual instruction is needed most and your help can pay the greatest dividends.

Part II

The Offense

4
Offensive Formations

One early decision that has to be made by any coach concerns the basic offensive and defensive formations he intends to have his team employ. The coach's experience and his personnel, the kids on his team, usually have an important bearing on this decision, but at the grade school level the inexperience of the bulk of the players limits the options. Thus, since the coach should be concentrating on teaching basic, fundamental football, the formations he employs should also be basic and fundamental. That is to say, simple. If the limited practice time is squandered on installing a variety of complex formations, fundamentals will suffer and so will the young athlete. More time and effort are wasted on fancy variations than they are worth, and the beginner team that does a few things very well will always beat the razzle-dazzle bunch that can not block and tackle.

Offensive line formations do not vary a great deal. Center, guards, and tackles line up the same just about everywhere. Some consideration might be given to the spacing between them, however, and this should be governed by what is needed in order to execute the plays properly. Usually a distance of about a foot and a half between the feet of adjacent linemen is a good guideline. Experimentation is recommended. But once the right distance has been determined it should be maintained by all the linemen every time they line up in formation. That sounds easy enough, but these youngsters are not known for their consistency and attention to detail and they keep forgetting to think very hard about how they are lining up. The normal tendency is to bunch closer and closer together until their feet are touching. This eliminates the hole, confuses the backs, and wreaks havoc on the play. Spacing between linemen must be stressed and consistency maintained during practice.

And how about the ends? The alternatives generally reduce to an ends keeping almost the same distance from the tackle as the linemen maintain, about a yard-and-a-half, or being split out wider, resulting in the terminology *tight* and *split ends*. The distance should be determined by the plays the team is going to run, but unless there is an unusually talented ten-year-old passer on the team, a widely split end will add little to the offense while decreasing blocking effectiveness. It is usually best to split one end about six yards, achieving the desired effect of spreading the defense and providing a wide receiver without losing a blocker. The other end should be no more than one yard greater than the normal one-and-one-half-yard spacing from the tackle. The terms *split* and *tight end* are popular with the kids and are good to use to designate the difference in lining up on offense, but in the youth leagues *split* and *tight* are relative terms. Another argument is likely to arise with ends who want to line up on the sidelines and run *fly* patterns. They will have to be convinced that it is not the distance that makes a split end but his primary role as a pass catcher.

Note that up to now nothing has been mentioned about "the formation" as an offensive system. The designing of a college or professional offense is one of the truly intricate mechanisms of producing an offensive attack. The positioning and movement of players within an offensive formation can and often do become very involved. If the youth league coach tries to imitate the trained and experienced big-time coaches with their trained and experienced big-time players he will create utter chaos. It is all the beginner can do to remember a few basic instructions without trying to have to figure out which offensive variation his team is employing on that particular play. As a rule, inexperienced linemen have considerable difficulty in trying to learn specific blocking assignments. They are trying too hard just to find someone to block, hopefully using proper fundamentals to move him in the right direction—away from the ball carrier. This is not meant to ridicule the young ball player but to point out the importance of keeping things as simple as possible. More specific assignments can be developed and incorporated into the offense as the youngsters are ready for them. Learning to block effectively should be what is emphasized, and it is very difficult, it takes time, and it should develop step by step, beginning as basically as possible.

Most formations today put the quarterback behind the center where he takes a direct snap. The lining up of the other three backs is what really determines the offense being used. The simplest formation is the "T," where all three backs are about two yards apart and about two yards behind the quarterback, ends tight. The "winged T" and the "slot-back" formations are earlier variations of the T that placed one of the halfbacks either outside the end or between the tackle and a split end. In either case he lined up closer to the line than the other two backs, usually about a yard behind the tackle or end. Currently three basic formations are used by most teams and probably present the average youth league coach with his most popular alternatives. They are the "power I," the "standard pro set," and the "wishbone."

In the standard pro set the two set backs line up about

where the halfbacks line up in the T formation. The other back is flanked wide to one side, and the end is split wide on the other side. In the power I both set backs line up behind the quarterback. The "up" back in a loose three-point stance is two or three yards back, the deep back with hands on his knees is another yard or two behind the up back. Again the

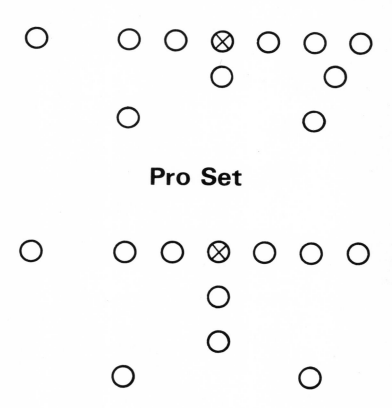

Pro Set

Wishbone

The common offensive formations

other back is flanked wide and the end is split. In the wishbone the fullback is about two yards behind the quarterback in a wide four point stance. The two set backs are two yards right and left of the fullback and about two yards further from the line of scrimmage.

It is important for coaches and interested parents at this

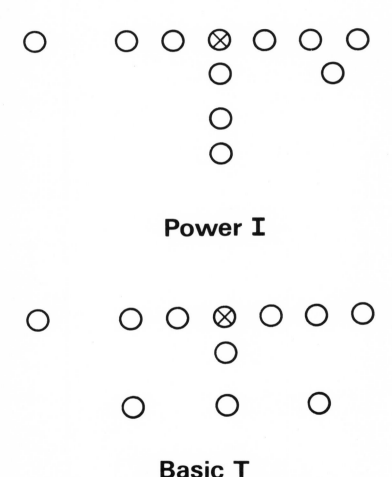

Power I

Basic T

level to understand that each of these formations is designed for specific results. The wishbone is a running formation that requires quickness and relies on the quarterback's ability to "read" the defensive tackles (guess whether their rush will be "inside" or "outside" the offensive tackle), capitalizing on a series of plays that key off of the straight-ahead power of the fullback and the quarterback option. It is a difficult formation to use properly and requires superior line speed and experienced ball handling. Both the power I and the pro set provide wide receivers on both sides (split end and flanker back) for a flexible passing attack. The power I, with its deeper set back, can be more effective on inside power plays, particularly for experienced running backs. The pro set is a little more flexible outside and provides more direct pass blocking.

Naturally the generalities mentioned above can vary with personnel and minor modifications. The basic question must be—what is to be achieved and what is available to achieve it with? Although the basic T is probably the best bet because of its simplicity, the kids want to identify with and will be very strongly in favor of the formations used by college and professional teams. An interesting compromise is to start with the basic T but flank the fullback just outside the end as a variant, calling it a pro set, with the fullback now called the flanker back, all other positions remaining identical. But whatever formation is chosen should be tailored to the abilities of the players and devised so that players can run their plays, adjusting the positioning to speed and timing. Then once the exact spacing and relative positions have been determined so that the play runs correctly, the formation has been determined. A final very strong recommendation: teams should limit themselves to one basic offensive formation with only minor variations, such as using a flanker to the right or to the left. A novice team will be better off spending all their time perfecting one formation than in dividing among several, each requiring a different approach.

5
Plays

By this time a team and its coaches have already given some consideration to the plays the team is going to use, because in determining the basic offense they were thinking about the players and their particular talents. All offenses are developed to make the most of available talent. The team with a good power runner, good passer, or good breakaway runner will tend to build the offense around what the star player or players do best. If the squad is entirely green and those talents have not yet manifested themselves choices are even simpler; start with the most fundamental and build as the team is capable of accepting new plays.

A lot of attention is given to the plays, and everyone has heard sportscasters talk about bread-and-butter plays or new plays for the big game. But in building an offense less emphasis should be placed on the play and more on play series because there is almost never a single play isolated from all others. It is too obvious. As the offensive game is developed everything must be incorporated into an overall game strategy. The defense is watching as the play unfolds and looking for keys to determine what is going to happen and where. Is it a pass or run? Right or left? Without elaborating on keys at this point it is necessary to understand that in putting together an effective attack, thought must be given to concealing from the defense what is actually taking place. That provides the quarterback the opportunity to set up certain plays and establish strategy.

Before going any further there should be agreement on a common frame of reference, identifying the back with the ball and the hole, or where he is expected to run. Beginning with the hole between the center and the left offensive guard call them consecutively one, three, five and seven, with the seven hole outside the end. Similarly on the right the holes will be designated two, four, six, and eight. The numbering of the backs is arbitrary and may vary with the formation, but for simplicity the discussion will be restricted to the pro set variation of the basic T mentioned earlier. Call the quarterback the one back, set back right (looking toward the defense) the two back, set back left the three back, and the remaining back the four back. Now specifics can be discussed.

The most fundamental series of plays from any basic T formation variation (which includes the pro set) begins with a straight-ahead play. In our formation this is either the left set back (three back) through the three hole or the right set back (two back) through the four hole. Let's create a series around the first of those, the three back through the three hole. The basic play is called the 3-3, identifying first the back then the hole. All plays in which the ball is given directly to the three back would begin with a three. Since it is a straight-ahead play it maybe referred to as a dive series. We could call it *quick opener* or anything else easy to remember. To further identify the series as developed around this play, let's call the series dive series left. This play, then, is dive series left, 3-3. The other play would be a dive series right, 2-4.

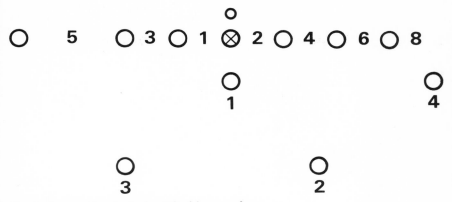

The holes and backs indentified by number

On a dive series left, 3-3, the three back drives straight ahead on the snap, takes a direct handoff from the quarterback, and moves up the field without a blocker. What do the other players do? To answer that will be identifying the other plays in the series. On any other play in the dive series left the quarterback will fake a handoff to the three back going through the three hole. So what are the logical options? *Logical*—meaning easy for the backfield to execute. How about the other set back slanting through the same hole? The quarterback could fake one handoff and make the other without moving. We could call that a dive series left, 2-3. Or perhaps the two back could sweep left end, dive series left, 2-7. We now have three plays in the dive series left, and since it would probably be desirable for the quarterback to block the first defensive man outside the offensive end on the 2-7, move him that way on the other two plays also, to give maximum deception. Another play in the dive series left might very well be dive series left pass.

What makes a series out of four separate plays is that the team executes the same moves, initially, on each play so that for a second or two the defense has difficulty in distinguishing one from the other. They are not sure whether the

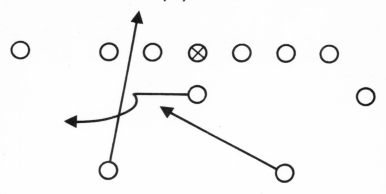

Dive Series Left, 3-3

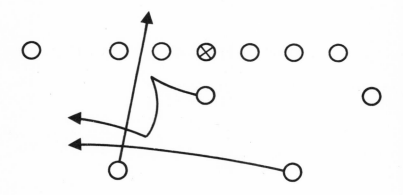

Dive Series Left, 2-7

quarterback is going to hand off to the three back or not. The blocking is different, of course, and the two back may make different moves, but initially they look the same, particularly

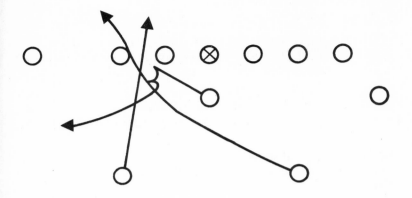

Dive Series Left, 2-3

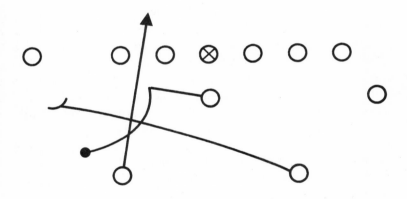

Dive Series Left, Pass

on the 3-3 and the 2-3. And other variations are possible. The quarterback could fake to both backs and hand off to the four back coming down the line and cutting over center, dive series left, 4-2, but that is a complicated play for beginners, requiring some time to execute. Similarly, the quarterback could fake handoffs and roll left or right, dive series left, 1-7 or 1-8. It is easy to see that the possibilities are almost endless, so much so that one series can have dozens of plays. And similar sequences can be drawn up for any hole and any back. The advantages of several look-alike plays should be obvious.

It is evident that in no time at all a team can accumulate a number of plays, and with each new variation the complexity of the offense increases without much effort—at least on paper. The secret to success is still execution without mistakes, and it is strongly recommended that both the number of series and the number of play variations within any one series be kept to bare minimums until those selected initially are learned and executed perfectly every time they are run. Do not teach new ones until they know the old ones. A newly formed team playing other teams at the same level can win with as few as three series with three or four plays in each series if they can perform without mistakes.

Which series to install and how to devise the plays within each series depends on what the team does well and is entirely up to the coach and his team. There is nothing really complicated about drawing up plays; the complicated part is adjusting the drawing so that it works smoothly on the ground. The simplest series are a dive and a power series. The dive or quick opener depends on a line's ability to open a hole quickly and the back's ability to get through it quickly. Interference blocking is not a feature, and everything keys off one of the set backs "diving" into the hole directly in front of him. A power series is probably the most direct of any series of running plays because of the lack of critical timing. It is also the oldest in football. It features a quick pitch or handoff to the trailing back and makes maximum use of interference blocking. Its beauty is that the variations consist of running the same play through nine different holes

46

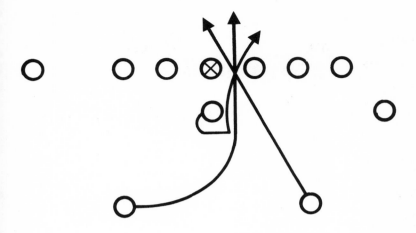

Power Series, 3-2

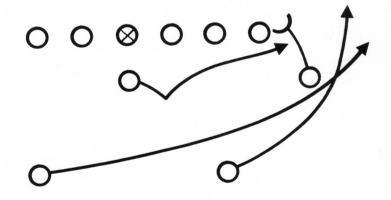

Power Series, 3-8

Variations of the power play

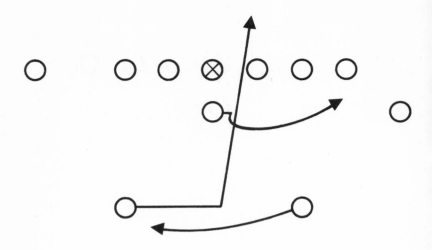

Dive Variation, 3-2

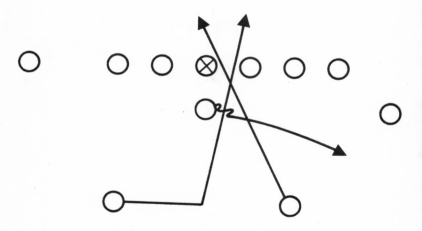

Cross Dive Right, 2-2

More dive variations

(directly over center is called the zero hole). It can be a straight-ahead power buck, an off-tackle power slant or cut back, or a power sweep with almost the same basic timing. Its shortcoming is that there is no deception whatever.

Some deception can be added to a power series by incorporating cut-back plays if desired. In fact, to develop an innovative series start with any play and then consider possible variations from it. Shown below are two more excellent basic plays that can be developed into series.

The third series would be a passing series. Although normal practice is to include one or more pass variations in each series of running plays, a team usually also has a pass option that eliminates the deception of faking a run and maximizes backfield blocking protection for the passer. The best basic pass for inexperienced players is a simple drop-back quick pass with the two set backs blocking. An effective variation of any pass series is the draw play, where the quarterback fakes a pass and hands off to one of the set backs who dives into the line.

The exact execution of the plays within each series is open to a variety of interpretations and will depend on the backfield formation and the players themselves. Series can include backs crossing, options, quick pitchouts, and reverses, but simplicity cannot be overemphasized. Several variations off one series are better than a new series, and good execution is more effective than variety.

Something might be said at this point about the relationship between positioning and the formation. The plays shown above are from a formation where the set backs line up directly behind the tackles, making a straight-ahead dive, either a 3-3 or a 2-4. If the backs line up in a tighter formation, say, directly behind the guards, the natural dive plays would be 3-1 and 2-2. Positioning of backs will be discussed within the basic formation later on, but it should be noted that their basic positioning as defined in the chosen formation is important and critical to the selection of plays.

As yet nothing has been said about line blocking assignments. That is not because they are unimportant but because at this level line blocking is best treated as a separate subject. Backfield assignments are obvious to the kids. A back can easily understand and remember what he is to do, and since the hole, which is defined by the offensive linemen, and the positions of the backs remain constant and are controlled by the offense the play functions pretty much the same in a game as it does during drill. That is not true with line play since the blocking assignments change with the position taken by the defense, making it very difficult for nine or ten-year-old linemen to learn blocking variations.

In order to keep their assignments simple it is best for them to concentrate on two things: where the play is supposed to go and when it is supposed to get there. For example, returning to the dive series, 3-3, the tackle and guard realize that the play is coming between them, and the first back through will have the ball. Each should know that he must block any defensive man opposing him away from the hole and that the hole must open quickly. If there is no defensive player opposite the guard, he blocks the linebacker. That is not very scientific, but if the inexperienced ball player can master that much initially and concentrate on good blocking fundamentals he will achieve better blocking than if he tries to learn and memorize intricate assignments that depend on how the defense lines up. What is important is that someone knows that he is to block the principal defensive players opposing the play. That is what practice is for. As the blocking improves and the players develop more experience, team blocking can be implemented so that on power plays and quick openers for short yardage two blockers can team up to block key defensive players. Maybe the unopposed guard would help the center, for instance, to block out the middle defensive guard. Trap blocking, switch blocking, and pulling guards should not even be considered until linemen demonstrate solid capability in one-on-one, straight-ahead blocking fundamentals. Plays can be altered and more specific blocking assignments made as the players' experience warrants it.

Play development is another area where parents can contribute to the team's success. If they haven't the time to go out with the team they may be able to help an inexperienced coaching staff a great deal by helping to develop a simple offense. Many youth league coaches will welcome such assistance.

6
Blocking and Offensive Line Play

Blocking is probably the most difficult operation for a young football player to learn, not so much because of the contact but because of the problems of maintaining contact and controlling the defensive player until the play is completed. More time will be spent in practicing blocking then any other single function of the game if the team is to be successful.

An interior offensive lineman begins from the three-point stance. On the snap signal he drives forward, head up, hands against the chest, elbows up, feet spread comfortably apart, taking driving steps. After making contact he holds this position with the shoulder and head, maneuvering the defensive player away from the play. It sounds easy, but it is not. Examination in greater detail will show why.

The initial drive was covered when discussing the three-point stance. But here are the points that should be stressed: (a) Keep the head and eyes up. The blocker must be able to track his target since it is not going to remain in one place. He cannot do it looking at the ground. (b) The hands must be kept tight against the chest. This is the rule. If they are not, the blocker risks a holding penalty. The teaching position is to keep the clenched fists against the front of the shoulder pads, forearms parallel to the ground, elbows up. In order to force kids to hold this position, it is often helpful to have them grab a fistful of jersey in each hand. (c) Drive to the target with a sprinting stride, concentrating on speed and quickness. (d) Once contact has been made, sprint through the target taking short choppy steps, keeping the feet a comfortable distance apart. This is important in maintaining drive and balance. (e) Keep the shoulders in driving position. Too many young players want to make contact with the chest from a straight up position. If the shoulders are not in a

The proper blocking position

position to drive into the opponent's solar plexus the block will not be effective. (f) Keep the knees flexed. This is important to provide the necessary drive and balance. Flexed knees will enable the legs to act something like a set of springs on a car.

Contact is phase two of the block and is an extension of phase one so that the body position does not change. The secret of good contact is proper placement of the head and shoulders and maintaining drive. If the head is positioned properly, the forward edge of the helmet and nose guard will drive against the opponent's chest. The blocker, knowing which way he wants to drive the defender, will then slide his head either to the right or left of his opponent's torso where, with the forearm and shoulder, he forms a wedge that he uses to move the defender. If either the head or shoulder and forearm are not locked in place the defender will easily slide or roll out of the block.

Follow through, phase three, adds nothing new but determines whether the block is effective or not. It is not good enough to make quick, clean contact if the defender remains in the path of the play. The object is to move him out of the way and make room for the runner. Head, shoulder, and forearm contact, flexed knees, and short choppy driving steps remain important in keeping the defender from regaining the initiative and moving back into the hole to make the tackle. The most frequent weakness in inexperienced blockers is loss of initiative. They should be taught to continue driving until the whistle blows the play dead, the defender is on his back, or the play has passed them—and then they should go and find someone else to block. Suggest to them that next time they watch the professional games on TV they should note how many times second effort makes the difference in the success of stopping a play.

These are the fundamentals. They must be constantly stressed and continually practiced in drills, scrimmage, and competition. The kids should begin with the tackling dummy, over and over again: head up, knees flexed, shoulders into the block, short driving steps. The dummy, incidentally, is an important piece of equipment and should have high priority in the competition for scarce youth league dollars. Once they can block the dummy they are ready to go against a yielding opponent who allows himself to be moved. Finally, they are ready for one-on-one against actively resisting opponents, where they will soon realize that things have become infinitely more difficult than they were in controlled drills. People are harder to block than dummies:

a) They move. When the defender refuses to stand still and be blocked, the operation is not nearly so easy, not that any of the fundamentals are changed but because they now have to be directed against a moving target who has ideas of his

The block—notice locked forearms (elbow out), flexed knees for drive, and position of head and shoulder.

own. The secret is to teach the blocker to keep his eyes on the target, knowing where he is and where he is going. And as long as he is not overextended and off balance he can adjust his drive to stay with his opponent's moves. Once contact is made the defender's movements can even be used against him, particularly if he takes one step in the wrong direction.

b) They do not stand upright. That tackling dummy was a big tall, straight-up target. A defensive lineman driving from a three or four point stance is something else entirely. It is fairly difficult for a blocker to aim his helmet at numbers when all he can see is the other guy's helmet. But again, fundamentals hold. With a good aggressive drive the defender will be straightened up, and once off balance can be driven out of the play. When the defender succeeds in getting lower than the blocker the situation changes a little because the blocker has lost the basic blocking position and therefore his control over the defender. But if the blocker continues to drive head, shoulder and forearm against his opponent, and keeps driving, he can pin him to the ground and keep him out of the play. The driving is still essential because without it an aggressive defender will push right under the blocker who is trying to lie on top of him.

c) They use their hands. Permissive use of the hands is the defender's primary advantage over the offensive lineman. He cannot hold, but he can push off and will try to use his hands to take advantage of the blocker's momentum, pushing or pulling him off balance. The blocker must be ready for the push and keep his balance in spite of it.

Downfield blocking is more difficult yet. The defensive down lineman has one primary function, and that is to drive forward in his zone of responsibility and contain the play. From the blocker's point of view this limits what can be expected and makes blocking easier. Downfield blocking, including a block on the linebacker, is complicated by the fact that the defender is not constrained to a forward rush but may be moving right, left, or backward. And lining up as much as several yards behind the line of scrimmage he can see the block coming and has time to react to it. Head up, balanced drive is the litany of the blocker, and for the downfield block is is more important than ever. A fatal tendency of even experienced blockers is to leave their feet once they have made contact. Another tendency is to aim the block at where the defender was rather than where he is. When the target is moving you have to lead it, and experience aids in gauging the defender's motion so the block can be effective. The offensive lineman should, additionally, always keep in mind the two advantages he has over the defense: he knows when the ball is to be snapped and he knows where the play is going. The first advantage gives him a jump on his opponent if he is quick enough and is concentrating. The second allows him to use the defender's momentum against him. Many times, the best way to move a defender away from the play is to help him keep going in the direction he is already moving. This will be covered in a later section when downfield blocking and the running back's use of a blocker are discussed. One point that should be stressed: the blocker should never assume that the defender is out of the play. He should make contact and hold it, ensuring that the defender is not able to come back and make the tackle. A quick defender can correct his mistake and regain his balance in time to recover and make the play.

The essential difference in blocking on a pass play stems from the rule that an interior offensive lineman may not leave the line of scrimmage until the ball has been thrown. That is a tough one to teach kids. A good guide for the blocker is to take no more than one step forward, and they may be taught not to step out at all. The pros will often take several steps backward, but that takes experience and balance and can prove disastrous to young players and their quarterback. In any event, pass blocking eliminates the drive and requires certain adjustments on the part of the blocker, too often resulting in stand up and bump even though it need not— because the fundamentals still apply. If he will stay low, keep his head up, forearms parallel to the ground, knees flexed, and legs driving or churning, the blocker will better be able to slow the momentum of the rusher. In fact, change in the momentum of the play is the big difference in pass blocking and requires balance on the part of the offensive lineman that must be anticipated and practiced. He should remember that when the play was a running play, both linemen, offensive and defensive, were driving and had forward momentum. In the pass block the offensive lineman surrenders his forward drive, and unless he has a size or strength advantage he will tend to be driven back; although if he will keep his legs driving it will help considerably.

The object of pass blocking is to protect the passer long enough for him to throw his pass. To do that it is necessary to develop a blocking pocket around the quarterback, something like erecting a curved human shield in front of the passer, keeping the defenders in the center from penetrating and forcing the others to the outside. The rule is—never let a defensive man go inside of the blocker. Doing that properly, however, takes a lot of team work and good fundamental blocking. Often, in order to hold the pocket, the tackles are gradually forced to give ground, moving back and toward the center. This leaves the center and two guards anchoring the middle with the two tackles turned outward, partly shielded by the guards. Whatever backs are assigned to block take up positions behind the tackles or end—if he is blocking—and are responsible for the defenders that manage to get around, most often the defensive tackle or blitzing linebacker who is trying to exploit a gap. The passer stands in the pocket formed by the line. If it works properly it should be like water rushing to each side of the bow of a ship.

The difficulty comes in trying to hold the solid front and keep the defense from penetrating. In the running play the blockers are trying to drive a wedge through a point in the defense. In the pass play they are trying to keep the defense from driving a wedge into their shield, and they do not have the advantage of being able to use their hands. Thus in pass

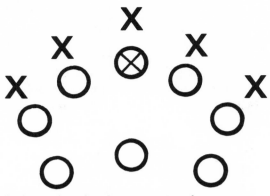

The correctly formed pocket for protecting the passer

blocking it is much more critical for offensive linemen to work together to keep gaps from opening between them. An inexperienced blocker will often become so preoccupied with his opponent that he will move away from his neighbor on the right or left, leaving a wide space through which the linebacker can shoot and make the tackle. Linemen must remember that since the defender has greater momentum than they do the blockers tend to be driven back. When that occurs the entire pocket must adjust, being prepared to be driven back, but as little as possible, with each blocker allowing himself to give some ground when necessary to maintain contact with his mate in keeping the defensive linemen from moving inside them. In a good pass offense the pocket will hold tight but move slowly back with the passer as he drops into his passing position. The teamwork required takes a great deal of practice, and that is the primary reason why a good passing offense is more difficult to develop with inexperienced players than a good rushing offense.

But beginners should not get the idea that pass blocking is the only place where teamwork is called for. Any time blocking occurs in the line players should strive for a cooperative effort. In fact, the youth league coach and his supporting parents should be constantly stressing to the young ball players that football is not an individual sport, and teamwork, team spirit, and working together are the very essence of any and all success. This is part of what makes football such a fine vehicle for teaching kids the basic principles of working together for a common goal, and parents with selfish motives can seriously undermine attempts at developing teamwork by feeding their sons' natural desire to gain individual achievement at the expense of team play.

As blockers mature and the offense begins to gel, it will become apparent that there are many occasions when the one-on-one block is not the most effective way to open a hole for the runner. Particularly on plays designed for short yardage in an obvious running situation, the team blocking or two-on-one can be preferable.

The team block takes special practice because the boys have to learn to coordinate their efforts so that they will not work against each other. Sometimes one will drive low, the other high. Other times both will execute normal blocks in such a way as to pin the defender between them, driving him out of the play. They can work out the strategy on their own, play by play, but should be cautioned to keep it simple. Because of his additional responsibility for hiking the ball it is often desirable to include the center in a team block on many running plays and even pass plays. A back can also take part in a team block. But care should be taken not to overdo team blocking to the extent that the linebacker is over looked and left free to make the tackle. Somebody must be designated to block the linebacker on each running play.

The simplest and first blocking drill is the one-on-one. The defender attempts to drive forward and the blocker tries to keep him from crossing the line of scrimmage, driving him away from the play. It is necessary to restrict lateral mobility in this drill because there is a tendency for the defender to, unrealistically, try to go around the blocker. Tackling dummies on each side, forming a corridor, are helpful and should be placed so that the only way to go is straight ahead. Use signals, with the blocker being told which one to start on. This does two things; it gets the kids used to signals and concentrating on signals, and it establishes offensive advantage, providing more realism. Here is a tip to save some time. Coaches standing behind the defensive lineman and giving the signal by a show of fingers works very well. He should then show him which direction to block by pointing left or right. The direction of the block should always be part of any drill since the blocker should always want to move his man away from the play.

Similar drills can be run with any combination of offensive and defensive players—two offensive and one defensive, three blockers and two defenders, all the way up to full offensive and defensive lines, with or without linebackers. This kind of drill becomes more interesting and more meaningful when a ball carrier is used but must be carefully controlled to keep the kids from getting carried away. When line and backfield are practicing separately and there is no back to carry the ball, the kids enjoy alternating ball carrying among the linemen, running straight ahead into the line at the designated hole. They have to be reminded: no fancy stuff allowed. This is a blocking drill and concentration on blocking execution is mandatory. Even though the kids are linemen, they still all want a chance at playing ball carrier and they can get carried away if they are not carefully controlled. The method of calling signals and designating holes by hand signals is still a worthwhile time saver when the clock is against a team.

This kind of drill can be lots of fun, but it cannot become a free-for-all. Coaches must always demand disciplined play and continually correct fundamental lapses. Of course, the final step is the controlled scrimmage, where two full teams are put together to run plays against each other. The players must understand a scrimmage is not a game. It is a controlled drill in which the goal is practicing fundamentals and sharpening plays against a full and reacting defense. If coaches are not present correcting mistakes, the scrimmage loses its value. Parents can help by explaining this to their competitive sons. All the kids want to do is play a game, and often they fail to realize the value of controlled practice drills.

The center in proper position over the ball . . . and in relation to the quarterback just prior to the snap.

Before leaving the offensive line a look should be taken at the specialized play of the center. His stance is the same as any other lineman, except instead of placing one hand on the ground in front of him he grips the ball with both hands, one exactly as the passer, who will be discussed in a later section, and the other on the opposite side of the ball to stabilize it. Some centers will grip the ball with one hand and place the other on the ground, knuckles down, like a guard or tackle, but this is not recommended for kids with small hands. They will never be able to control the ball. As the other linemen, the center should keep his weight balanced between the hand and the balls of the the feet but with more weight on the feet. There is no need to try to look back between his legs, and his eyes should focus as the other linemen at a point about a yard in front of him.

The snap is straight back and up so that the quarterback can grasp the ball with his spread hands. Note that the quarterback grasps the ball, the center does not place it in the quarterback's hand. All the center does is place it in the same position every time. Signals are particularly important to the center since if he is off everyone is off. Using the hut-one, hut-two signal sequence, the center snaps the ball on the hut, not on the number. Practicing regularly with the quarterback to get the snap down perfectly, the center should learn to anticipate the count ever so slightly, requiring steady and even cadence by the signal caller. Blocking by the center is identical to that of any other lineman.

Hiking the ball for a punt requires additional practice. Since the object is a good, hard, spiralling, and accurate pass, the center usually looks at his target between his legs and passes the ball much like a passer, picking it up and snapping it back all in one quick, smooth motion. It needs to have a good spiral and should be aimed at the kicker's numbers. The whole operation must be drilled very much like a passing drill for accuracy and consistency, first without opposition and then under pressure. A muffed punt because of a bad snap can change the entire complex of a game.

7
Running and Ball Handling

To run full speed toward someone and crash into him without flinching is not natural. Some people can never do it. But it is something that every good back must learn because even though he probably will not be running over defenders on every play his overall effectiveness will depend on his ability to do it when he has to . This requires some early consideration on the part of would-be backs, their coaches, and their parents. Kids should try to play positions they are adapted to, if possible, and one of the early questions is—who is going to play in the backfield?

It seems that nine out of ten kids want to play one of the back positions so they can become another O. J. Simpson, Joe Namath, or Larry Czonka and sign multiyear, multithousand-dollar contracts. Do not think for a minute that they are ignorant of contracts and glory. Ours is that kind of society, and even at ten years old many of these youngsters are already nurturing dreams of college scholarships, pro contracts, and television. But choosing the backfield players is a big first step for any youth league team. Who gets the job? What is important? Speed, size, agility, ball handling, intelligence, coordination? These are the basic attributes of any ball player at any position, and the coaches have to balance talent among line, backfield and defense.

Probably the most important abilities a back can illustrate are keeping his balance, accelerating quickly, and being able to put his head down to drive. The dancer who fears contact will never make it. Youngsters will invariably point out that flashy pro breakaway backs like Mercury Morris and Greg Pruitt make their yardage by tricky broken-field running; but ask them what they do when they are hemmed in. Every one has the capability to put his head down and drive, and the defensive backs know it. If a boy runs hard and does not hesitate on contact he will be a good inside threat. If he also has speed and quickness he is a potential star. But everybody does not have these attributes. In fact, there are very few who do. It is a wise parent who evaluates his or her son early in the game and helps him select a position where he can achieve his maximum potential. If he is not a back the parent can help him by showing him the advantages of playing another position.

In the early stages of team development members of the backfield should work by themselves for a portion of each practice session. This is not to say they should not take part in blocking and tackling drills, because they must. But they need time to get the feel of each other and of the offensive system. At this juncture of a young ball player's growth his ability to *handle the ball* and "handle" the offense is significant to a quarterback hopeful. He should, additionally, be able to pass adequately, but the ball handling has to come first. In the youth leagues running must come first because a team may be able to run without an effective passing attack where passing without a running threat is much more difficult.

The backfield should be trained on the first play of the

primary series, usually a power play or quick opener. In order to concentrate on the handoff, method of carrying the ball, acceleration, drive, and timing, all three running backs should alternate in the ball-carrier position. When the coaches are satisfied with each back's performance in running that play they should add the counter play or first variation and again let each back play the ball-carrier and faking-back positions. By the time they have these two plays down cold they will have an understanding of what the offensive requires, and who should be starting in each of the backfield positions will usually be evident. But in a youth league a coach has to be flexible because his players move away, quit, get sick and sometimes simply do not show up for practice. If coaches are not prepared for that they will come to practice one day and find that they can no longer field an offense. But, of course, parental interest and support can help influence that as well. Optimally, a team would have two full backfields and one or two spare backs. But often the number of kids available or the number of uniforms the team can afford makes that a luxury not too many enjoy. It is also important that the defense not be weakened at the expense of deepening the offensive backfield, although most kids will learn to play both ways during the first several years. In fact, they should be encouraged to play both until they really know what position to concentrate on.

The first step in learning to play the backfield is instruction on how to carry the ball. Everyone knows how to carry the ball, they will say. That may be, but if you watch an instant replay on a fumble you will find more often than not that the ball carrier was careless and not carrying the ball correctly. He should hold it so that one end is between the forefinger and middle finger and the other end is wedged firmly into the armpit, elbow tight against his side. Problems arise when he deviates from this basic position. The "loaf of bread" is the classic. Here the ball carrier fails to make sure one end of the ball is tucked firmly into the armpit and it squirts out with a gentle tap. Another typical mistake is made by quarterbacks who try to absorb a tackle with the ball held as if about to be passed. But probably the problem that most frequently leads to a fumble occurs when the running back is carrying the ball correctly and trying to avoid a tackle. The tendency here is to use the arms to maintain balance, and when the elbow is not held in close against the body the ball becomes vulnerable. The teaching point is—always keep the elbow in. But in maintaining balance in the open field that may not be as easy as it sounds.

From the very beginning it is important to stress exact positioning, each back knowing where he should be on every step of every play and aware of his relative position with

The correct ball-carrying position: one end tucked into the armpit and the other between forefinger and middle finger.

respect to the other backs. For a play to go smoothly, precise positioning and timing of movements must be consistent. This takes a lot of practice. When learning the play, kids should first walk through it so that each back may have the opportunity to get the feel for exactly where he is to go.

Next comes the ball exchange. The first exchange is from the center to the quarterback, and it is an important one that is too often overlooked or taken for granted. The tendency is for the quarterback to start to move before making sure he has complete control of the ball. He should seat it firmly against his stomach before he moves. An inexperienced quarterback should practice this at home over and over again until he can do it in his sleep: snap, grasp, hold. It is a drill that is not nearly as exciting as passing so it tends not to get much attention. But that should not be allowed to happen. If there is not a clean exchange between center and quarterback the offense is off to a bad start. While practicing the snap, quarterbacks should be instructed to call signals and pivot each time. That way the snap, pivot, and seating of the ball tight against the stomach becomes a single, smooth motion.

The simplest quarterback handoff, the next exchange, is executed by holding the ball with both hands, the hand nearest the line flat along the ball, the other at the bottom tip, guiding it. The relative position of the hands change depending on whether the quarterback is pivoting right or left. The ball carrier will hold his hands so that both forearms are parallel, fingers spread, with the hand in which the ball is to be carried under the other. The quarterback will then lay the ball in the cradle of the ball carrier's arms and hands. Note that the quarterback *lays* the ball in, he does not slam it in. This is usually best accomplished by having the quarterback hold the ball stationary with the ball carrier grasping it as it touches his hands.

An integral part of any handoff is the deception that should

The quarterback handoff

accompany it. In order for the play series to be effective the defense should have difficulty in determing when the ball is being handed off and when it is being faked. The quarterback's body should be in such a position as to shield the handoff as much as possible from the defense, and the hand and arm position of the running backs should be the same whether they are taking or faking a handoff.

The most critical part of ball handling, however, is timing. This is where practicing plays, first at half speed, then at normal speed, pays off. Split-second hesitation by the quarterback, the ball carrier, or the faking back can and will spell the difference between success and failure. And the only way timing can be insured is by practice.

Once the ball has been handed off to the running back and the blockers have opened a hole in the defensive line, it is up to him to exploit his advantage. And again timing and quickness can be the difference between a touchdown and a two-yard loss. Too often a youngster will want to make sure everything is in order before rushing in. Although that is a good approach to most things it does not make great running backs.

The play begins with the snap. In some plays it may be necessary for a back to hesitate for a count or to take several deliberate steps away from the play before cutting and running seriously toward the line to achieve the right timing. But when he begins to run he must run hard and accelerate quickly. Also, the tendency to hesitate while taking the handoff deprives a back of important momentum, and when there is no hole or when it closes quickly that momentum is very important.

"Running to daylight" is an often-heard expression that is appropriate to discuss at this point because it is often misunderstood and can be another excuse for not running hard. Many inexperienced backs think running to daylight means once they get the ball they should look to see where it appears to be open and run in that direction. That may work in backyard touch football, but it spells disaster in organized league play. Teamwork, again, is the key. When every player devises his own ideas there is chaos and nothing works. The running back's job is to take the handoff and run for a given hole. If he does it right he does not even have time to look around for daylight. But once into the hole or through it, that is when he should start running for daylight.

What does that mean? By the time the back "hits the hole" the play has begun to unfold, the defense is in the process of committing itself, and the blocking pattern has taken form. Each time the play is run, depending on how the defense reacts to it, the pattern may be a little different. After crossing the line of scrimmage the opening may be to the right, to the left, or straight ahead as a result of the actions of the linebackers and deep backs. The ability to perceive these openings without breaking stride is the mark or an effective open field runner. The Otis Armstrongs and Franco Harrises of the NFL have made an art of continual adjustments to "day light," and the power I was created to provide the best opportunity for them to do it, but always without losing momentum.

This phase of running is hard to teach because instead of hard and fast rules common sense and instinct prevail. But there is one guiding principle that endures. The novice back should be taught that he has one "cut" and one cut only. Once he is through the line he makes the decision and sticks with it. Otherwise he will be hesitating or dancing and his momentum will be lost. As he gains experience he will better understand what that means.

There is another aspect of running with the ball that must be covered, and that is the proper use of a blocker. The opportunity to use a blocker occurs mostly on wide plays or open-field situations where the play has time to develop. In such cases the ball carrier is accompanied or led by a blocker or blockers, referred to as "interference." The defender, with his eyes on the ball carrier, wants to dispatch the blocker and make the tackle. In the process he will normally attempt to push the blocker aside, and when he does he commits himself, giving the blocker an angle on him that the ball carrier can use to break loose. Often a feint by the back to one side can help the defender make up his mind to commit, setting up the block and leaving the ball carrier clear sailing to the other side. The term *angle,* is the positioning of the blocker to place himself between the defender and the ball carrier.

This takes time, however, and sometimes the runner has to slow up for the block to set properly. Whether that is advisable or not is a matter left to the judgment of the ball carrier. With strong interference the guideline is usually—

stay with it. With a single blocker and strong pursuit any slow-down more than the slightest hesitation to set up the block is not advised, particularly when the reinforcements are close at hand. Like running to daylight, use of a blocker improves with experience.

The final phase of the run comes when there is nowhere to go and the runner is faced with contact. How he reacts at this point is very important because of the possible, extra, vital, few yards, and a player can develop a reputation that gives defensive backs the respect that can also convert to extra yards. The tendency among the timid or inexperienced is to try to pull away or step aside from a tackle, and occasionally that might work; but more often it will result in an opportunity for a gang tackle and often a fumble. The most consistent ground gainers are the ones who put their shoulder down, lift their knees up high and drive straight ahead, downfield into the would-be tackler. The knee action in particular should be emphasized because driving knees both intimidate the tackler and provide added drive and momentum.

When to drive and when to cut or fake? When to use a blocker and when to leave him and set off solo? Only experience will really teach the running back how to react in a given situation, and much experience can be gained in running drills. Drills should be emphasized over scrimmage in youth league play for reasons that relate to the inherent limitations at this level. A scrimmage should be monitored closely, requiring sufficient numbers of experienced or at least knowledgable and forceful coaches to watch each aspect of play and make on-the-spot individual corrections. Too seldom does the neighborhood yield adequate coaching talent to provide offensive coordinators, line and backfield coaches, defensive line and back coaches, and so on. Consequently, if a team concentrates on drills to develop the experience and uses scrimmages to put it all together, they will gain the best use of the limited time and talent. Player shortages also lead to this solution. Drills such as left side defense against right side offense (with a full offensive backfield) allow simulation of actual playing conditions, running plays only to the right. When there are not two full teams for practice this type of expanded drill provides scrimmage conditions with advantages of fundamental drill and tighter control. And, finally, in a drill you can create more precisely the situation necessary to train the new player in specific areas of weakness.

Good open-field experience can be gained in setting up a block by placing the defender about five yards from the sideline, ten or fifteen yards upfield from the blocker and ball carrier, and starting action on a whistle. The ball carrier, led by the blocker, will have to decide whether to stay on the inbounds marker or cut toward the center of the field. A variation starts the ball carrier ten yards in from the sideline, running laterally across the field, cutting at the sideline. This requires him to make a downfield cut and is a little more challenging. Leading the ball carrier as before, the blocker lines up exactly where he did in the basic sideline drill. Two defenders or drill without a blocker are additional variations. Obviously, there are any number of combinations of players that can be used in a live action drill and any number of situations that can be simulated, depending on what a team is trying to practice and how large a segment of offense and defense are needed to simulate the situation desired. The essential points are: a) it must be kept realistic, b) it cannot be allowed to get out of hand, and c) it should be kept as simple as possible.

Now to return to discussion of what really makes the running play work—timing and consistency among plays in the same series. As has already been observed, timing is the critical factor in successful play execution. The offensive backfield is a machine, a team within a team yet part of an eleven-man offense. In order to click, the offensive players have to learn to act like a machine, executing their moves smoothly and consistently. During necessary backfield play drill, the stress should be on timing and consistency as well as on correct execution. Once the backfield unit has learned the play thoroughly, players should always run at full speed, just as they will in a game, so that the timing will be perfect.

Sometimes it will be discovered after running a play several times that the timing is not quite right because one back is just a fraction of a second slow and cannot get to the right place on time. This is not unusual and with young players can even develop halfway through the season as a result of the tremendously rapid development that can take place with boys this age. It may require slight adjustments to the lineup such as "shading" the back a half step left or right when he lines up on that particular play or having him "cheat" forward a half step or so. These changes are too small to be readily discernable to the defense but can make the difference between a play running smoothly and always being a little ragged. A team must be flexible and willing to experiment, and the kids can and should be allowed—indeed, encouraged—to contribute ideas. But once the coaches decide on the adjustments it should be understood they are set and should be run the same from then on. If a later change becomes necessary coaches should not hesitate to make it but must make sure that a player does not make it on his own without everyone realizing that he is doing it. They cannot be experimenting on their own if it affects timing. The result is the mental and physical discipline mentioned earlier.

The other important aspect of team play in the backfield that leads to successful execution is the carrying out of assignments. What is expected of the ball carrier, has been discussed in some detail but it is equally important that the other backs carry out their assignments just as diligently. That is what makes the play series effective. If the dive and the crossbuck in the cross dive right, for instance, look identical to the defense, they will never be able to key on either one. And for the two to look identical each back must do the same thing on each play of a series—whether he has the ball or not. The quarterback has a particularly significant role in the deception, and if he just waves the ball at the faking back he will fool no one. He must learn to actually put the ball against the faking back's stomach and take it back again without fumbling, and, obviously, the more effective the fake the more chance there is of fumbling. So it must be practiced over and over again.

Before leaving the running play a brief examination of some different types of plays and some factors that make each work successfully may be valuable. Backs always line up the same way in a given formation to avoid "tipping off " the play, usually in a loose, three-point stance with almost no weight resting on the pivot hand. Exceptions are the quarterback, the fullback in the wishbone who lines up in a four-point stance for quick straight-ahead acceleration, the fullback in the power I who stands with hands on his knees so that he can see over the up back, and the flanker who may stand straight up, adding deception to his intended pass pattern.

A straight-ahead power play, dive, or quick opener requires the set back to accelerate quickly, developing good speed and momentum by the time he gets to the line. The difficulty he experiences when he does it right is that it all happens so quickly. The quarterback must have the ball ready to hand off, and the running back must develop acceleration yet be in the right body position to take a handoff, all in the space of three yards and about one-half second. Anyone who believes the dive play is the simplest in football to execute is not running it right. Simple in concept and simple in execution are two different matters. And the full-speed handoff is the difference. It is the key and it is difficult.

A slant play or cross buck eases the pressure on quick acceleration but poses new problems in positioning. On an outside slant (the play slants away from the middle) the quarterback must make sure he moves out to where he can effect a smooth handoff. On an inside slant there is increased danger of collision, particularly when the two backs are crossing. These plays depend on the backs' taking great care to run the play exactly the same each time so that positioning is precise. A slant play also requires the ball carrier to make a decision at the line of scrimmage since the play will develop differently if he continues diagonally toward the sideline or cuts up field. During play drills he should make this decision, consciously, every time he runs the play.

Some plays employ a cut in the backfield rather than a slant. These plays usually develop like a sweep and then turn into a power play when the ball carrier makes a right-angle pivot or cut. Slipping is a danger if it is done carelessly, and positioning is critical since a back out of place can cause a collision or a missed handoff.

The sweep, to be effective, must get the ball carrier outside. The team in an early development stage that can run a sweep effectively has a very powerful weapon. But it is not as easy as it looks. The problem too often encountered is that the play becomes ponderous and develops so slowly that the defense is lined up in depth on the sideline by the time the runner and his phalanx of blockers arrive in the "flat." Quickness is important on a sweep, and for that reason many teams employ a quick "pitch-out," which has the advantage of quick movement to the outside but the disadvantages of limited blocking and vulnerability to fumble or interception of the lateral pass. A good power sweep teams a back moving quickly toward the sideline and his blockers, sometimes including a running (or pulling) guard. The blockers must be just as quick as the ball carrier so as to be able to keep ahead of him and get outside the defensive end and linebacker before they can react to the flow. The success of a sweep depends on the block of the halfback or flanker on the first man outside the offensive end. And the most critical time in the sweep is at that point where the ball carrier converts

76

lateral speed to downfield speed or when he "turns the corner." Too often young backs are unable to make this move quickly enough and in "rounding" the corner lose their momentum. Using the blockers and gauging the flow of the defense are also important. This is where that key block on the first man outside the offensive end comes into play. If he can only be blocked out, toward the sideline, the ball carrier may have to cut inside. If he is blocked inside, and this is preferable, the runner cuts outside.

A popular razzle-dazzle play is the reverse. It is always dangerous to employ because it requires the ball to change hands several times and takes time to develop. But when successful it can be electrifying. The typical reverse play begins as a sweep and brings back either the flanker or the end against the flow, wide around the other end or cutting inside, up the middle. The play seldom works more than once in a game and should not be considered for addition to the offense until several good solid series have been learned thoroughly and should not be used in a game until the basic series of which it is a part has been successfully employed. The reverse requires a great deal of practice in timing and handoffs between running backs. Double reverses normally require too must time to unfold and are too complex for developmental leagues.

Finally, there are the rollout and the option plays, which, with the sneak, make up the quarterback's running repertoire. The option is much like a sweep, but the quarterback keeps the ball and has the option of cutting over tackle or lateraling to his trailing back. It is a key play in the wishbone offense and takes a cool and confident quarterback. It is also extremely dangerous for the same reasons that the quick pitch is dangerous. These plays take practice, experience, and more than a little ability in ball handling. The rollout may be either a quarterback sweep with three backs blocking or a naked run where the blockers run one way and the quarterback rolls back the other way. Both can be very effective variations when employed as part of a series with a strong running quarterback, but both have drawbacks. The sweep is difficult to develop quickly enough to get outside and usually looks very much like an old-fashioned single-wing power sweep: whichever side is physically stronger prevails. The obvious problems with the naked rollout are the lack of blocking and the need for deception and surprise.

8
Passing and Receiving

Passing is a highly personal skill even when a player is only nine or ten years old. Often by the time a strong-armed youngster has reached that age and decided to embark upon his career in organized ball he has already developed a personalized style from father, uncle, or a neighborhood athlete, and it is probably best for coaches not to change it. By trying to do so they are likely to do him more harm than good. Parents should exercise some control over what he learns; if they allow him to learn mistakes in passing, coaches are not likely to change them.

There are some good guidelines for passing where a coach or parent should concentrate his efforts. The grip, for example, is important. Generally a passer will grip slightly behind the center of the ball, with the tips of the fingers on the strings. But the firmness of the grip is what is important, firmness and consistency, so that the feel of the ball is the same each time and the chances of having it slip prematurely are minimized. Regardless of how experienced he thinks he is, the budding young quarterback should spend some time practicing his grip until it becomes habit.

Once he has the grip the next step is to be sure he can make the ball go where he wants it to go. Accuracy in passing does not just happen. It comes from long practice. Usually a straight overhand delivery contributes to passing accuracy, beginning with the ball cocked behind the ear and ending with a forceful overhand snap. Delivery is the key to accuracy and depends on control and timing of the release, both of which respond to diligent individual practice. A drill for the off-season is to work on throwing at a target such as the proverbial auto tire hung from a rope tied to the branch of a tree. The passer begins close to the target, perhaps ten yards, and passes with the tire stationary. As he progresses he can vary distance to the target and finally pass at the tire swinging.

When grip, delivery, and basic accuracy have become steady and consistent he is ready for human targets. To begin, anybody will suffice as long as he gives the passer the feeling of a moving target. But during the season he should concentrate on his regular receivers since timing is influenced by individual speed and personal moves. As in the development of an effective running game and blocking, timing and teamwork are the basis of a successful passing combination and the pass play must be as carefully planned and developed as the running play. It is not an accident that professional pass receivers seem to be right where the quarterback expects them to be.

Whereas a running play is built around the movements of the various backs, the pass play is built around the movements of receivers—running patterns. As in developing running series, a team should also develop passing series, one at a time, concentrating on each member of the team doing the same thing each time the play is run, laying the groundwork for critical timing between passer and receiver and deception. A major difference between the two types of plays is that a single pass play is in itself a variety of options depending on the moves of several potential receivers.

The guide for inexperienced ball players must be to keep the patterns as simple as possible so that the receiver can

The ball cocked behind the passer's ear—the proper ready position for the overhand delivery.

learn and practice just a few basic moves, and the passer is not burdened with more than he can handle. Three patterns, completely mastered and deceptively executed, will create an effective pass offense at this level of play. They are sideline (or flat), look-in, and buttonhook. Each begins with a receiver running straight downfield.

The buttonhook or curl pattern requires him to "hook" at first down distance downfield. A look-in or over-the-center pass requires him to cut or pivot—instead of stopping—and run straight across the field parallel to the offensive line several yards behind the linebackers. On a sideline or flat pattern he does the same thing but cuts toward the outside.

Pass-pattern development on a given play should be designed to confuse the defensive backs trying to cover the potential receivers and take advantage of the fact that the passer and receivers know what is going to happen and the defense does not. This is where timing plays such an important part since if the receiver executes his move well the defender will lose a step or two, leaving him open momentarily. If the ball is thrown right at that moment, chances for a completion are very good. Ignoring the receiver for now, several things relating to the passer should be stressed.

The first to remember is that pass blocking and the development of a pocket are difficult. So it will be an unusual situation when a team consistently provides more than three seconds of protection for a passer. This means that even in passing drills the quarterback should get rid of the ball in three seconds or less. Sometimes counting off the seconds out loud is helpful. Generally the most efficient use of those few seconds is for him to take two or three quick steps straight back, stop, set, and look for his receivers. The steps backward cannot eat up more than one of his seconds, so he will have to use that time to get his grip on the ball and set quickly. That gives him another second to pick out his receiver, and that should be plenty of time if he knows where the receiver is going to be and he is there. It is evident that it takes a great deal of coordination and timing drill to get it just right. When the pass play is a variation of another series such as the dive the passer's positioning for the pass must be integrated with the fake of the running play. This also should be fit into the three seconds.

Some passers will backpedal in dropping back, keeping their eye on the potential receivers without making it obvious to the defense. Others will turn their backs on the line, run back, turn, and set, hiding the ball and giving the defense the momentary illusion of a run. Each has advantages and disadvantages. Poise of the quarterback, blocking, and prescribed patterns will be influences on which technique he will employ, and he might even want to use different techniques on different plays. A drop-back passer, for instance, has to use the other technique on a pass from the dive series.

Three seconds is not much time. For the receiver that means he should allow himself one move and one move only; no dancing, no running all over the field. He should go straight out, make his cut and look for the ball. For the passer it means he should already tentatively have selected in his mind his primary receiver, the first man for whom he will look, even before he has turned and set. If he is covered, the passer will look for the alternate receiver, and that is usually all he will ever have time to consider. A third receiver's function in the youth leagues is to confuse and spread the defense and add a third variation to the pass play. The blocking difficulty being what it is, a third receiver may be an expensive luxury, and the team might be better off keeping him in to block. The folly of more than three receivers should be obvious. When the receiver has been selected, timing the release with his moves becomes the essence. The pass should be thrown and the receiver looking for it immediately after the cut.

As players progress to more sophisticated levels of football, passing attacks will become considerably more complex. Blocking will improve, the quarterback's time will increase, and players will be able to handle more receivers and more complex patterns. But during initial learning stages if a team has any hope of mounting a passing offense it must be kept extremely simple and plays must be executed quickly. Three popular patterns that have not been mentioned are the fly pattern, crossing pattern, and a screen. The fly, where a receiver runs straight down the field deep, requires a very strong and accurate passer, a fast and talented receiver, and time. The crossing pattern is a deep slant over center, and also requires time. Usually, long passes at this level are rushed and thrown high toward the vicinity of a receiver where they are up for grabs. The screen requires experienced linemen and some relatively advanced blocking experience. Another pattern or variation is the flare, where one of the set backs hesitates and "flares" out into the flat, toward the sideline but still in the offensive backfield. If executed properly a flare can be a good play, but it pulls one of the blockers and only works at this level if unexpected. Another possibility is a flare by the end, which can work if coverage is loose and the pass is thrown quickly to the opposite side from what would be expected from the flow of the play.

Depending on the maturity of the team, two options are open in calling pass plays in the huddle—set plays or improvisation. A team can either have set combinations—short pattern one (the team knows that the left end and wingback both buttonhook)—or the quarterback can designate the patterns he wants in the huddle: drop-back pass, right end sideline pattern, wingback curl, right set-back flare, on two. It is probably best to begin with two or three set combinations and allow the quarterback to call variations as the team is ready to handle them. But this point should be understood: players should not make up patterns as they go. Any improvisation must be restricted to assigning which set pattern will be run by a given receiver.

Before leaving the subject of pass plays mention must be made of one more essential weapon in the pass offense, the draw play. This is a play that looks like it is going to be a pass but is instead a delayed run up the middle by a set back who feigns a block and, as the quarterback drops back, accepts a handoff and executes what amounts to a delayed dive play through a designated interior hole. Blocking differs from the normal dive play since there is a delay for which the linemen have to be prepared. Deception and surprise are also extremely important since the delay deprives the runner of momentum. A draw should be designated as any other running play by back and the number of the hole, such as a 2-2 draw play. But it is employed as a variation of one of the pass plays. As a matter of routine plays should be designed so that the quarterback will fake a draw on a pass play.

This is a good opportunity to show the importance of a series concept. Consider what was said about the technique used by the passer to drop back. The draw is easier to run with a quarterback who turns his back on the line in dropping back because the handoff is easier to execute and it is hidden from the defense. The passer who faces the line and backpedals has to turn around to make the handoff. In either event, whatever he does on the pass he should do on the draw to make the play work effectively.

The success of a passing game rests on two essential conditions—the success of the running game and the effectiveness of pass blocking. If a team cannot mount a running attack the defense can lay back and wait for passes, making life much easier for them. If a team cannot protect its passer his ability is academic. But if those two conditions are met the ability of the passer becomes the key ingredient to success. His poise is very important, and passing drills under pressure can help him develop it. A rattled passer is likely to make costly mistakes that must be avoided.

The first is failure to set. The quarterback who tries to pass before he has both feet set on the ground is not going to be accurate, and this does not only occur when he is being rushed hard. Many youngsters have difficulty in remembering to set first and must be continually reminded. Another typical mistake comes when the passer tries to throw the ball before he has a good grip on it. Finally, there is the passer who will throw even when there is little likelihood of success. The passer who throws into a crowd or to a receiver who is well covered is forcing the pass and will be intercepted often. If the receiver is not clear the pass should not be thrown. Some practice time is normally devoted to drilling the quarterback on action to be taken when his receivers are covered. A good approach, going back to the three-second guideline, is—during passing drills the passer should occasionally check his receivers, one at a time, then tuck the ball under his arm and drive into the line. He must have a feel for the three-second timing so that he can gauge his actions accordingly. Not that there is anything automatic about three seconds, but it provides a planning guide, training the young, inexperienced quarterback that he must be prepared to run when his receivers are not clear. If he learns to take off before he gets hemmed in he can avert losing a lot of yardage. But it takes timing and awareness.

As in every other aspect of the game of football, passing demands teamwork, and the other end of a passing combination is the receiver. Potentially there are five of them, two set backs, flanker or wingback, tight end, and split end or wide receiver. If all were used at any one time it would reduce the potential blockers to the five interior linemen and leave the passer very vulnerable. But as the passing offense develops each may at one time get the opportunity to run one or more of the basic patterns.

The first impediment to a receiver is the problem he may have in clearing the line of scrimmage. The tight end is usually involved in blocking the man opposite him, and any of the other receivers are liable to be "bumped" by the opposition to slow them down. With only three seconds available to get clear and have the pass in the air this delay can be very costly, and the receiver has to avoid becoming involved at the line.

Once clear of the line he is free to run his pattern. The first leg is usually straight down field, trying to "face up" on the defensive back (attempting to run straight at him). He will usually run between five and fifteen yards, but that does not mean the receiver decides how far he runs on each play. The pattern specifies how far he runs, but there may be deep and short variations. However, when a pattern is called in the huddle both quarterback and receiver should know exactly how it is going to develop. This is not easy to teach inexperienced players because as the defense adjusts and linebackers get in the way they tend to want to revert to their backyard touch football habits and dance around to get clear. It does not work. Football is a game of discipline, and when players begin doing their own thing a team can fall apart rapidly. This does not mean that adjustments cannot be made. It means that if they are—say, the short sideline pattern is causing the split end to consistently get bogged down in traffic—they may be changed, and the end may run two or three yards deeper. But it is done as a coordinated effort by a team and not on the whim of the receiver while he is running the pattern.

To make it easy for the learning receiver, his distances downfield should be defined by a number of steps or in terms of yard markers, if the team is fortunate enough to have a marked field, until he gets a feel for the distances. This will initially be cumbersome but it is the only way most kids will get to understand the importance of exact patterns. An instruction such as, "when you get behind the linebacker . . ." is no good because it can become confusing when the linebacker lines up in unorthordox defenses or drops back to cover the pass.

The next phase of the pattern is the pivot or cut. And an integral part of the pivot is the fake. If the defense knows what is coming, the job of defending becomes much easier, so faking or deception can be an important part of most patterns. When the receiver hits his pivot (plants his foot to cut) he wants to keep the defender in suspense as long as possible and would like to make him think that he is going to do something different than he is actually going to do. As in the play series for a run, until the pivot has actually been made, the sideline, look-in, and buttonhook should all look like exactly the same pattern. That is how the receiver gets clear. He causes the defender to hesitate or even commit himself a step or two in the wrong direction, thinking that that is the direction he is going.

On the sideline pattern the receiver makes his cut toward the sideline by planting the foot farthest from the sideline and changing direction from downfield to laterally. It is a quick right angle change of direction using the yard stripes to run toward the sideline. On the look-in pattern he does just the opposite. The curl or buttonhook is different in that the defender should not be prepared for the receiver to stop. When he hits the pivot on a curl he should turn around quickly and take a short step back toward the line, facing the quarterback with his hands set as a target. Each pattern should look identical to the defense until the move has actually been made.

The fake on the pivot is accomplished with head, eyes, shoulders, and sometimes hips. These are the "moves" that distinguish an effective pass receiver, and they require practice and imagination. Deception can be gained by taking a step in the wrong direction with the pivot foot; or by throwing the hip, shoulder, or head opposite the intended direction of the cut or merely looking in that direction, shifting the eyes to confuse the defender. What is important is that the moves not becomes stereotyped and that they do not detract from the immediate goal of getting to where the quarterback expects him to be within the three seconds. Multifakes or fakes that slow the cut are worse than none at all, and a receiver who always looks left and cuts rights fools no one. His cut should be his first concern. If it is quick and clean the inexperienced defender will have trouble staying with him anyway. Faking is a refinement that comes with experience and should not be forced.

Immediately after making his cut the receiver should be looking for the ball. For the best timing on a quick pass, the quarterback is anticipating the cut and will be starting his delivery as it is being made. This is where counting and timing are essential. It takes a lot of practice. But it is all wasted if the receiver cannot hold onto the ball. Catching is done with the fingers, not the arms or chest. Just as in properly controlling a basketball, the football is caught with and held by the fingers. A high pass should be caught with the hands placed

The receiver ready for a pass

so that the thumbs are together. A low pass, at or below the waist, should be caught with the hands placed with the little fingers together.

Several things can happen when the ball arrives on target that can keep the pass from being a completion. A common mistake occurs when the receiver allows his attention to stray from the immediate task of catching the ball. Sometimes he is so anxious to run with it that he starts downfield before making the catch, taking his eye off the ball. Then, sometimes he is painfully aware of the defender coming up to cover him and becomes more concerned with getting hit than he is with catching the ball. The defender also has something to say about whether the pass is completed or not. Two things a receiver must learn early with regard to the defender. First, he must always keep his body between the ball and the defensive back to guard against interception; second, he cannot worry about being hit when he catches the ball. A good defensive back who knows that he cannot get to the ball will time his tackle to just the moment the ball arrives in the receiver's hands, jarring it loose. It is something anyone who wants to catch passes must learn to live with, an occupational hazzard among receivers.

There is yet one more step in successfully catching a pass—running with the ball. When the ball has arrived at the target the receiver grips it firmly with his fingers and tucks it under his arm, covering the ball with the other hand. This is done in a single, smooth motion, and while it is being done he turns and drives downfield. All receivers should be trained to practice properly seating the ball and driving downfield on every practice catch. Catch, tuck, cover, and go. It is the part of pass catching too often glossed over. It must become habit.

Putting it all together is a matter of practice and developing teamwork. During passing drills the receivers should always run established patterns identical to those in the play series. Even if they are not the intended receivers they must strive to run good patterns partly to practice deception and partly because next time might be their turn. To add complication to passing drills it is often worthwhile to place defenders in the opposing backfield. However, they must play the positions honestly. Their most important function there is to give the receivers an opportunity to learn to ignore their presence and concentrate on the ball and the pattern. Like hitting a baseball, catching a pass is a function of hand-eye coordination and concentration.

Part III

The Defense

9
Defensive Formations

An interesting aspect of professional football over the years has been the tendency of either offense or defense to gain ascendancy for a short period of time only to be reversed during the next phase. Player development goes through the same kind of cycles and initially defense has the edge. More specifically, the youngsters find it easier to learn defensive play than offensive play because during the learning process it is easier to keep something from happening than to make it happen. Stated differently, during the learning phase the offense makes a lot of mistakes and the defense can achieve considerable success by standing by and letting the offense beat itself. Besides, even a sloppy tackle can bring down a weak, nonaggressive ball carrier, and it.is easier to elude a block than to execute one.

That is all the more reason why correct fundamentals must be stressed with first- and second-year players. The first phase does not last long, and if players find themselves successful without applying good fundamentals they become lazy, complacent, and laden with bad habits, and when the offense catches up they have difficulty unlearning them. If they have not learned correctly, they will not know what to do when they face an offense that has stopped beating itself.

Defense in football has progressed from something you had to do between times you had the ball to a specialty requiring the best an athlete has to offer. It has been said that if a player can play equally well as a running back on offense and as a cornerback on defense a professional team will always play him on defense because of the relatively greater challenge of that position. Be that as it may, defensive play has become a highly complicated and technically demanding specialty with multiple variations, switches, and combinations.

As with the offense, defense for beginners must be kept simple if they are to be able to concentrate on learning how to play football correctly. A youngster faced with remembering a series of complicated defensive maneuvers will inevitably slight the fundamentals and lose the opportunity to build good basic habits. One method utilized by some leagues to force fundamental development is to either limit the defensive options or specify a standard defensive lineup in the league rules.

Regardless of the defensive formation used a team should concentrate on straightforward and relatively rigid player responsibilities. As the individual players develop, these responsibilities can be expanded but should start out as simple as possible. The responsibilities will depend on the formation but should stress a good aggressive rush, fighting off the blocker, and good clean tackling, which will be covered in detail in a later section. Each line position should begin with a single basic assignment and each backfield position one assignment for a running play and another for defending against the pass. How can a defensive player limit himself to a single assignment when there are a whole series of different offensive options that require different responses?

94

The function of the line is to contain the play and limit the offensive options. The tendency of an untrained player is to either allow the play to deteriorate into a personal confrontation with the opposing lineman or to embark upon an equally personal pursuit of whoever happens to have the ball at the moment, thinking that he is the only player available to make the tackle and that he must do it all by himself. By now the reader should know what follows. As seen repeatedly, the first and greatest lesson of football is that it is a team sport, and players must always remember they are working together toward a common goal. In the case of the defense that goal is to stop the play from gaining yardage.

Each defensive lineman must be assigned an area of responsibility. The formation will determine what it is, and how each player handles it will be discussed later. But in the early development two critical responsibilities for defense against the run must be defined and understood: wide responsibility, who is responsible for keeping the play inside; and how the team is going to stop it once it is forced inside. The youth-league team that cannot keep the opposition from running wide will achieve little success.

The need for simplicity and the importance of developing an effective defense against the wide run will create an early dilemma for a team of weekend television fans. During the 1930s the most popular defenses featured a six-man line because it was effective against the wide run. Today you see concentration on three and four "down" linemen because the potent threat is the pass. Normally youth football relies heavily on the run as the most consistent offensive weapon because, as discussed, running attacks are easier to develop than passing attacks at this level. But the kids want to emulate their heroes and they should learn formations that convert easily as they progress to higher levels. So what should they do?

Probably compromise. But it is done with an understanding of what is being done and why. It is easier to contain wide plays with an end than with a linebacker because an end can

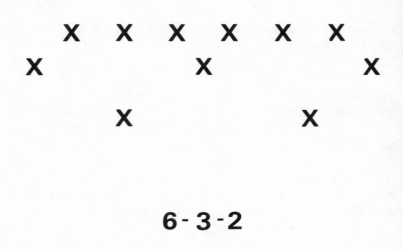

6-3-2

5-4-2

Some defensive formations

catch the play before it has developed. Thus the six-man line is preferable. But the desired affect can also be achieved with a five-man line, and if either end is designated to rush, the linebacker must assume outside responsibility. As for the

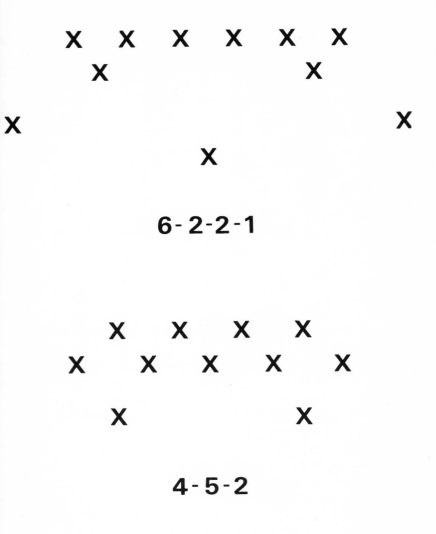

6- 2-2-1

4- 5-2

rushing linemen, each down lineman should be given responsibility for any running play that comes into his assigned area, whether a quick play, a delay, or a reverse.

Linebackers are responsible for providing back-up support to the line in containing the running play but must also be prepared to defend against short passes. The traditional six-man line used two or three linebackers. With a five man line either three of four linebackers can be used. Unless your team opposes some pretty unusual ten-year old passers the defense will have to concentrate on the run and the short pass, which suggests maximum strength in linemen and linebackers and minimum at the deep back positions and weights the decision heavily in favor of a 6-3 or 5-4 configuration. With four down linemen a team would probably want to use five linebackers.

The deep secondary, so critical in the college and professional ranks, becomes less important in development leagues due to the normal lack of an accurate long passer who has time to set and throw. Even if he does have the capability he seldom has adequate blocking to provide the time he needs. Thus the concentration of nine players at the different combinations of line and line backer positions is effective in the youth leagues, leaving two deep backs to defend against the long pass and provide deep back-up against the run. If the young defensive backs press to use a free safety or roving back it should be resisted unless there is a player with enough experience to be able to diagnose the play and consistently be in position to be on top of it. Such a back can sometimes play a roving linebacker position and make real contributions. Linebackers and deep backs must also be assigned areas of responsibility so that if a rover is used the other linebackers divide up the area to be covered. If there are three of them one usually covers anything between the offensive guards, the other two from the guards outward. The rover back does not have an area but adds defensive depth wherever he plays. A popular term for him several years ago was ''monster man.'' A final recommendation to any inexperienced team is to keep variations very simple. If variations are used and those variations change basic defensive responsibilities, confusion can develop.

10
Defensive Line Play

Defensive linemen assume a stance much the same as offensive linemen. As they mature and develop their own styles, however, many tend toward a more elongated, spread-out, four-point stance. The reason for this is that while the offensive lineman is primarily concerned with balance and ability to adjust, the defensive lineman is more concerned with straight-ahead drive. But in the initial stages the fundamentals are the same and the same points—placing the feet and hand, keeping the back parallel, drive, balance, and looking where he is going—should be stressed.

There are differences in play, however, and one of the most important is that a defensive lineman is allowed more liberal use of his hands and arms. This is the defensive advantage that balances the offensive jump resulting from knowing on which count the ball is to be hiked. But this advantage is not unlimited and has to be explained carefully and monitored during practice. Use of the hands does not permit holding. It permits flat-handed pushing or pulling, and the distinction is worth fifteen penalty yards.

The "front four" (or front five) have specific area responsibilities, as already discussed, with each man concerned with any running play attempting to penetrate his territory, and the passer on a pass play. The seven interior holes (zero through six) are divided among them. Each lineman positions himself directly in front of an offensive lineman and on the snap of the ball drives straight ahead, controlling his area. The positioning is significant because to the inexperienced player it looks as if it would be much easier to rush *between* the offensive linemen rather than directly at them. But remember what the blockers are trying to do. As the play comes toward the line each offensive lineman is intent on driving his opponent away from the ball carrier. By choosing the gap the defensive lineman makes it easier for the blocker to move him away from the play going the other way. If he guesses right he still gives the offensive man an angle on him and a good ball carrier will sense the block and slide away from the already committed defender through the now-open adjacent hole.

The advantage of taking the blocker straight on is that it keeps the defender uncommitted and in control of his area. If the blocker attempts to move him left he resists the pressure and drives right, diagnosing the direction of the play by analyzing the attempted blocking flow. And this is where the hands can be used effectively. The blocker, in leaving the set position, develops momentum in his initial drive. By using the hands to push or pull him in the direction of his momentum the defender can easily send a poorly balanced blocker sprawling.

Stressing the area responsibility is important in developing interior defensive linemen. One habit that detracts from effectiveness must be broken early, and that is the tendency to become involved with the blocker, to allow the one-on-one situation to end up in a personal contest. That is exactly what the blocker wants. The defender's only interest in the blocker is to get him out of the way so that he can control his territory without interference. But in the process he finds out from him what he needs to know about the play. He does this by reading pressure. His motto should be *hit, read, and pursue.* It is also important that the defensive lineman have a good working knowledge of basic offensive plays so that he can recognize the difference between a quick opener and a delay; so that he can "feel" a cross-buck developing; and so that he is not caught unprepared by a reverse, draw, screen pass, or trap block. He has to realize that too aggressive a pursuit can leave his area of responsibility wide open for these plays.

For several years in the player drafts, Oakland's number one consideration for linemen selection was lateral speed. Their concern? Stopping the opposition from being able to run wide. At any level it is important to contain the outside running game. If the opposition can consistently get outside and gain on wide running plays they have a dangerous advantage. This is particularly true in early development leagues, where the ball carrier has a clear edge in the open field due to the inexperience of tacklers and the difficulty of executing a one-on-one open-field tackle.

The outside is an area, just as the seven interior holes make up areas, and responsibility must be assigned. Normally in college and professional strategy, the down linemen do not have outside responsibility. Contrast this with the old single-wing 6-2-2-1-defense where the outside responsibility was the sole prerogative of the defensive end. The essential difference is that current offenses almost always have a dangerous passing threat to contend with, whereas the single-wing offenses were heavily run-oriented. The goal in developing your defensive players must be to prepare them to play against modern balanced attacks; yet the key to the offensive attack in youth leagues will be the running game, and if the opponent can run wide he will have the defense on the ropes.

The compromise approach suggested earlier is to use a

five-man line and assign the two ends primary outside responsibility and outside linebackers secondary responsibility. This trains the linebacker but does not put the whole load on his shoulders. The center guard covers zero, one, and two holes; the tackles, three, four, five, and six holes; the ends, the outside. Ends line up on the outside shoulder of the tackle on one side and outside either the end, tackle, or wingback on the other side, depending on the split. On the snap of the ball they drive *straight ahead* about three steps and *read,* being prepared to turn inside to force the play toward the middle. Their instructions should stress the initial forward drive and the necessity to get outside the play, placing them in position to turn it in. There is a strong tendency among undisciplined defensive linemen to gravitate toward the middle, causing a hefty traffic jam, all in a knot, leaving openings to the outside. It takes constant emphasis in practice to convince youngsters, particularly the ends, that they should penetrate straight ahead into the offensive backfield and avoid stacking up over center. But even in penetrating they must read and remain alert to slants and reverses that delay into their zones. What it boils down to is that each man has a job, and if they all do it right the opposition will find it hard to run. Once again, it is the team effort that succeeds.

11
Tackling

The keys to good tackling are aggressiveness and desire. Just as with blocking or running, there is something unnatural about deliberately smashing into 90 or 100 pounds of moving bone and muscle. Some find quickly that it can be a really satisfying experience. Others never learn to care for it. And that is the first real point of separation between good defensive football players and the rest of the pack. A normal youth league team may find one or two players who are not initially tackle shy, and the coaches will do their best to train the rest to understand that "he who hits hardest hurts least." One advantage in starting young is that a player learns the fundamentals at an age when the other guy is not yet sufficiently developed to cause him serious physical harm. The little guy doing the hitting and being hit will not believe that, but it is true.

It is necessary to be able to make tackles under a variety of circumstances in order to play good defensive football. But the place to begin is the direct and uncomplicated head-on tackle, where the ball carrier makes no attempt to elude. If possible, it is even better to begin with a tackling dummy. Just as with blocking, this gives the beginner a chance to get a feel for what he is doing without worrying about anything but the elements of a good tackle.

And, as in blocking, the aiming point is the center of mass, the old breadbasket, right at the base of the numerals. The tackler should move in a balanced position, feet spread comfortably apart, knees bent, and head up. Sound familiar? As he drives his forehead into his target, wrapping his arms around the ball carrier's hips, the head will slide to one side or the other and the shoulder pad will sink into the pit of the stomach. It is important in trying to avert injuries that kids not try to take the full impact of the tackle on the head and neck, so the sliding off of the head is a significant part of the tackle. It should be evident that the fundamentals of a good tackle are almost identical to those of a good block except that instead of holding the arms against the chest they are free to wrap around the ball carrier. And as in blocking, a successful tackle depends heavily on the follow-through or drive. The momentum of the ball carrier will almost always carry him over a stationary tackler and a single bump will just divert that momentum in another direction. So in order to be effective the tackler must match the ball carrier's momentum with his own drive, achieved by keeping the knees pumping.

This can be emphasized in drill by having the tackler run in place, bringing the knees up high, keeping his feet spread apart, before actually making the tackle and then emphasizing keeping the legs driving after contact has been made. He should do it first on the dummy, staying with it until the idea has become firmly implanted in his mind. If he absorbs that point it will be worth all the time spent on it, and he will have a "drive" mentality. When graduating to an actual ball carrier it is important that the drill remain fundamental. This can be achieved by restricting the play to a narrow corridor.

Two tackling dummies, laid horizontal about three feet apart will channel the action, confining both ball carrier and tackler to a straight-ahead confrontation that permits no dancing and no maneuvering. The player with the greater momentum will prevail. This drill is good for ball carriers as well. An interesting variation begins with both tackler and ball carrier lying on their backs head to head. On the whistle they go at it in the same manner. It is particularly beneficial in teaching the need for quickness since the fellow who moves too slowly gets clobbered. Fundamentally, open-field tackles are no different from head-on tackles, but since the ball carrier is free to change direction the former can become considerably more difficult to execute. Stress should be

The correct tackling position: legs balanced and driving, head to one side, shoulder pad making contact just below the numerals.

placed on keeping the head up, feet spread comfortably apart for balance and drive. These points are even more important in an open-field tackle since it is necessary for the tackler to be able to move with the ball carrier. There is a tendency to want to set for a tackle. Even when their feet are in motion they set themselves, losing flexibility. They must understand that the balanced boxer's stance and the driving legs have to be coupled with a flexible mental attitude that prepares them to move laterally. They cannot permit themselves to adopt a waiting attitude. Once the tackler becomes rooted in place the ball carrier has all the advantages of mobility and momentum.

The fumble recovery

Another facet of a ball carrier's moves is necessary for the tackler to understand. Since feints are performed with the head, hips, and shoulders, the tackler must train himself to concentrate on parts of the anatomy that are more reliable, specifically, the torso or the numbers, the center of mass. A good tackler, with the capacity to move laterally, will be able to ignore the fake and stay right with the ball carrier's illusive moves while making a good, clean, driving head-on tackle.

Although not at all confined to the defensive line or tackling, this might be a good place to mention fumble recovery. Almost everyone experiences problems with recovering a fumble because the unusual shape of a football makes it bounce in strange ways. The recommended way not to recover a fumble is to try to pick it up. It can be done, but more often than not this results in disaster. Another method not recommended is to fall on the ball. Essentially, what young players must learn is to lie down beside it and cradle it in their arms, quickly. It takes practice and fumble drill is a must. It should be done on a whistle, first with the ball lying dead, then bouncing. Youngsters will learn that it is not easy. One other consideration: players must be taught to be fumble conscious. Any time there is a loose football whoever becomes aware of it should yell "fumble" or "loose ball," so that everyone knows that it is loose and will be looking for it. Incidentally, it is best to decide on one or the other. Whatever warning word is used should be a signal to everyone, triggering an automatic response. Fumbles are important turnovers that must be exploited, and unless the player is aware there is a loose ball he may be totally oblivious of it lying at his feet.

12
Defensive Backfield Play

The basic difference between offensive and defensive play is that good offensive football requires flawless execution and good defense proper reaction. *Read and react* is the key defensive thought. It is more difficult to practice defense because coaches can only provide guidelines and try to instruct the defensive ball player, and particularly defensive backs, on developing the instincts that are so important to effective play. This is primarily why the defensive coverage in this book is less detailed than the offensive coverage.

Among defensive backs the linebacker is unique. Half lineman and half back, he requires assets common to each and must be adept at stopping both passing and running plays. If linebackers are weak so is defense, particularly in the early development stages. Whereas a lineman has a relatively narrow area of responsibility and is primarily concerned with straight-ahead drive, the linebacker ranges laterally over a broader area. The basis of his play is mobility and balance, and his initial stance reflects both. With feet spread comfortably apart, knees flexed, head and hands up, and eyes on the near-side offensive set back, the linebacker lines up about a yard behind the line of scrimmage. He is the back-up man, a sort of mobile reserve. His first instinct must be to remain uncommitted until the play has unfolded to the extent that he knows where it is going to strike and can move to assist the lineman in making the tackle on a running play or cover a short receiver on a pass play. This is the "reading" of the play. The stand-up position and the location behind the line give him a vantage point where he has a better view than the linemen, and his hands are up and ready to fend off blockers.

Beginning with the setting of the offense, the defensive back begins analyzing the play, and with the snap the first broad diagnosis is, pass or run? His priorities: play the pass first, then the run. The linebacker's keys are the offensive line and near-side set back. By watching the set back, he apprehends his initial indication of the flow of the play. By simultaneously "feeling" the offensive line, he gets immediate indication as to whether the play is a run or pass. Recall the restrictions on the line blocking for a pass play. Again, if there is any question, his first reaction is for the pass, then the run. Since blockers are limited to a maximum penetration from the line of scrimmage, blocking on a pass is significantly different from blocking on a running play. On a pass, blockers tend to straighten up and there is a noticeable absence of downfield blocking. This difference should be apparent to the defense without actually watching any one lineman. But a properly executed draw can be deceptive.

The linebacker has specific responsibilities on a pass play that vary with the team's coverage philosophy, zone or man-to-man. And while linebackers may have coverage responsibility on a short receiver, they must also be prepared to protect their zone in the event of a draw play or when the quarterback is unable to find a receiver open and has to run.

As with defensive linemen, linebackers divide the field of play among them. Four linebackers will normally cover from

The linebacker's proper ready position . . . and in relation to the defensive lineman in front of him.

center to tackle and from tackle outside on both sides. With three linebackers, the outside two cover everything outside the one and two holes. The use of a rover back has already been discussed. The play of linebackers can differ considerably depending on the variety of defenses, experience, and style, but beginners should concentrate on basic fundamentals.

It is generally felt that if a team can control "the middle" it controls the game, and for this reason inside or middle linebackers can be the most important players on the defensive team. Chicago's Dick Butkus was a case in point. This is less obvious in developmental leagues because of the tendency to bunch in the middle, clogging the center holes, and highlighting the criticality of the outside threat. But the inside linebackers working with the center guard will determine whether a team can consistently gain on straight-ahead power plays and quick openers.

A cardinal rule is—resist the pressure of the block. Using hands to ward off the blocker while keeping head up to watch the play, the linebacker tries to move laterally to the threatened area, being particularly sensitive to which way the blockers are trying to move him, fighting against the block. The challenge can be clearly demonstrated by the comeback play or inside reverse where, while the flow of the play is toward the outside, the pressure of the block on the linebacker is directly the opposite. If he follows the flow and moves toward the outside he sets himself up for the block and leaves his area unprotected. By sensing the pressure away from the middle he can diagnose the play and be where he wants to be.

The play of the outside linebacker differs chiefly in the expanse of his territory. Having a lot more area to cover, he must be mobile enough to act like a deep back and tough enough to stop up an inside hole. An outside linebacker always has outside responsibility. Even if the end is instructed to remain outside the play, wide responsibility

Use of the hands in avoiding a block

remains with the linebacker. That pertains not only to modern defense, but also to developmental leagues, excluding the old 6-2-2-1. Where the job becomes difficult is at the point where a back running wide has to make his decision whether to go outside or cut back over tackle. The effective linebacker, playing off the block while realizing that the back is doing the same, has to know when to ride the play out to the sideline and when to drive quickly into the inside hole. If the linebacker has sole outside responsibility or the end has been eliminated from the play, he must stay outside, keeping the ball carrier on his inside shoulder and also denying the blocker the opportunity to get an outside angle on him. Timing is important, but teamwork with the tackle, end, and deep back is vital. He should be intent on tackling the ball carrier but if unable to do so should make sure that he deprives him of his interference and leaves the deep back a straight shot. Defensive backs should be taught from the very beginning that they are not alone and should always know where the other backs are on every play. Talking to each other helps a great deal.

Defensive backs other than linebackers—called halfbacks, cornerbacks, deep backs, safety men, or free safeties—have one of the toughest jobs in football. They must be fast enough to stay with the fastest receiver, quick enough to adjust to the moves of the cleverest faker, and strong enough to bring down the toughest running back in the open field. This is not as critical in a developmental league, however, because of the relatively weaker deep-pass threat. If the opposition cannot throw an effective "bomb" the most important function of the deep back is to back up the linebackers and team with them to defeat the quick pass and provide last resort against the run. But it is always dangerous to preclude the long pass from the expected. The deep back's first concern is the pass, and even more than the linebacker he must remain uncommitted until he is sure that the play is not going to be a pass. Even then, since he is the final man in the defense, he should be careful not to commit himself before he is sure where the play is going.

A big consideration in higher levels of football is whether to employ man-to-man or zone defensive coverage of pass receivers. Most college and professional teams use a combination, and coverage is both complex and difficult. In the youth leagues, that must be simplified and either one or the other selected.

In man-to-man an approach is to assign one deep back to each wide receiver. Once the pick-up has been made he stays with his man wherever he goes. Any other receiver is picked up by one of the linebackers, depending on his positioning. The right set back, for instance, might be the responsibility of the left outside linebacker. The linebacker also stays with his man wherever he goes. Another approach is to let the deep backs take the first two men out, with linebackers taking the delayed receivers as they come out. This coverage may vary with the defensive formation and can be beaten by a sophisticated passing attack but can be effective in a developmental league. The key to man-to-man is that once a back picks up a receiver he stays with him wherever he goes.

In a zone defense each back is assigned a zone, and he is responsible for any receiver who enters his zone. When the receiver leaves one zone and enters another, coverage responsibility changes. A simple zone defense is the three-deep zone where the field of play is divided into thirds, the first within five yards of the line of scrimmage, the second from five to fifteen yards, and the third everything else. Backs are given responsibilities within these zones. Another approach would be to designate zones for each back corresponding to their areas of responsibility discussed earlier. Zones must be well defined, however, and switching coverage drilled.

Whichever coverage is used, an area of required emphasis will be linebacker coverage, particularly where a receiver pulls him away from his zone and the play is a draw or reverse into the zone vacated. This requires quick reaction by both the linebacker and the deep back as soon as they have realized the play is not a pass.

Some specific pass plays worthy of mention are the flooded zone, the safety valve (trailer), and a fly pattern. The flooded zone sends three eligible receivers into the same flat. This can overtax a zone defense but is no particular problem if each receiver is covered by a defensive back responsible for him, although they must be alert for it. The safety valve or trailer can be more of a problem because the flaring halfback may drift out opposite the flow of the play and must be covered by a linebacker who resists chasing the play, being mindful of his area of responsibility. The fly, especially when three deep receivers are used, can create a real problem for a young team unprepared for it. Requiring a strong passer, this play sends the two wide receivers straight down the field and crosses another over the middle deep. The third receiver becomes the responsibility of a linebacker who has to drop back into the middle to cover. Of course, an aggressive line with a hard rush is the secret to destroying the bomb and is the best possible defense against any pass.

These and other specific plays must be dealt with individually, and it is often necessary for the defense to adjust to a threat that is causing problems. In fact, each new game will probably call for adjustments to the defense. But once again, adjustments are made by the defensive unit and the coaches coordinating as a team—not on an individual basis. The "blitz" or "red-dog" is kind of a built-in method of adjusting. In a blitz one of the backs, linebacker or halfback, abandons his backfield position and rushes as a lineman. It is a gamble because it leaves his area open and it requires double area coverage by one or more of the other backs. However, it creates surprise and can be very effective if used properly, meaning not too often and when a pass play is expected. If permitted, it should be practiced and coordinated with only one back rushing at any one time. The blitzing back is designated in the defensive huddle, and the other backs adjust accordingly to the gap he leaves. Some time should be taken by all defensive backs to practice against the different possible offensive pass patterns so that they will have worked out combinations to deal with them.

Instructing a defensive back on the fundamentals of his position is not an easy task because his play is so dependent on reading and reacting. A first consideration is to resist early commitment on a play. The backs have additional reaction time because of their deeper positions and they should use it, keeping options open until the course of the play is firmly established. Part of this is the rule that he plays pass first, then the run. Once committed he gives the advantage back to the offense, and a wrong move by a deep back can result in a touchdown. Another rule is—never let the receiver get behind him. A defensive back should always try to keep a receiver between himself and the passer. Initially, most backs will pick up coverage by backpedaling, watching the receiver and keeping a corner of the eye on the passer. Denver's John Ralston claimed that his 1975 first-round draft choice, Louis Wright, could backpedal faster than some players can run forward. If the receiver is flying it becomes necessary to turn around to stay with him, preferably one step ahead, watching the receiver. That should be emphasized. When the defender can no longer watch both receiver and passer he should stay with the receiver and concentrate on his eyes. He will give an indication as to when the ball is in the air, and when he signals that he is going after it, then the defender looks for it too, keying on the receiver's reactions.

Many times, if the receiver is keeping his body between the ball and the defensive back and timing of the pass is good, it is difficult to get into position to intercept or knock the ball away. The prescribed action in this case is to time the tackle so that contact comes at exactly the moment the receiver touches the ball. It often works very well, and even if the ball is not dropped the receiver has no opportunity to run with it after the completion. But if the timing is wrong and contact is made before the ball arrives interference is called: automatic first down for the offense. This should be taught cautiously and practiced extensively before authorized for use in a game because it is not easy, it requires experience, and it can be expensive when the back is overanxious, which is so often the case with younger kids.

Playing the cut and the fake is another difficult task for a beginning defensive back. He should keep the receiver between himself and the passer and concentrate on the center of mass, maintaining a wide stance to permit moving right or left with the cut. The cut takes time, so a balanced defender with ability to move laterally quickly can stay with it—

provided he remains flexible. Consider what might appear an inconsistency. Do you watch the eyes or the center of mass of the receiver? When he is maneuvering for position it should be the center of mass. When he is in a position to make the catch and the defender is not in position to see both the receiver and the ball it should be the eyes. The best guidance to a young defensive back is be flexible, and *think!* Be aware of the entire play and what is happening—not just right in front of him but all over the field. And when he sees something the rest of the team should know he should yell it out, "pass," "reverse," or "fumble," using a consistent set of warning words so that there is no question of misunderstanding. Young players must learn to play as a unit in the defensive backfield, always working together, talking to each other and sharing confidence in each other's ability. And backs have the view to be able to see what is going on. That automatically puts them in a position where it is their duty to provide leadership.

Putting It All Together

This discussion has been of offensive and defensive fundamentals. If a young, would-be ball player were to master everything covered herein, he would be ready to start learning to play the game of football, meaning that he has to learn to put the fundamentals into game format, and only by experience will he really learn to play. There has been no attempt here to delve deeply into the details of sophisticated coaching techniques. In fact, the object has been just the opposite—to avoid details and concentrate on what everyone—coach, player, and parent—should know. Details come later. But some guidelines are also needed on the preparation for making that big step from practice to the game. Before looking at them, it should be made clear that the serious football player is a dedicated student of the game, and as such owes it to himself to go from here into more detailed coverage of the fine points of the play of the quarterback, the running back, the linebacker, or whatever position he is interested in. Each is a study in itself, and books have been written on the specifics, the sophistication of play, position by position. Trap blocking, pulling guards, and zone defense have been mentioned, but all but the briefest discussion avoided. Many other aspects of the game have not even been mentioned because to do so would detract from pure fundamentals and go beyond the scope of this book. The game of football is not simple and it should be studied just like any other complicated subject, expanding from a solid fundamental base.

Kids watching football on television or at the stadium pick up many pointers and probably have a good general idea of how it is played. But if this is their first season of actual play they must be given some instruction on the rules. Every player and his parent should read the rule book. But that is not very realistic for a nine-year-old boy. Here are the basics that he must understand as a minimum before going onto the field under game conditions.

—There are four quarters in a game and each lasts eight, twelve or fifteen minutes depending on the level of play. An official keeps time on a stopwatch, and the team captain and coach should always be aware of how much time remains. Game strategy is heavily influenced by time, and the captain or coach can ask the official for the time whenever he wishes. There is a break after the first and third quarters, and play continues where it left off after switching ends of the field, changing the direction each team is facing. At the half there is a rest period and play begins all over again.

—Another aspect of time beginners have to understand concerns the limit imposed on a team in getting the ball in play. From the time the ball has been "spotted" to when it is hiked can be no more than twenty-five seconds or there is a five-yard penalty. This means that the huddle must be efficient and organized.

—Penalties are awarded for improper play. "Offsides" means that a player is not lined up completely on his own side of the line of scrimmage or that he crosses the line before the ball is snapped. "Motion" means that an offensive player is moving before the ball is snapped. A back may be in motion provided it is not toward the line of scrimmage. A back who shifts must be still for one full second before the snap or he is guilty of "illegal shift." The same penalty can be called on a lineman who moves at all after he has assumed the set position, and that is one infraction against which some training is required because many defensive players will jump to try to get the offensive man to move. The defensive lineman is permitted to move around; the offensive lineman is not. "Clipping" is blocking another player from behind. "Holding" is assessed against a lineman who holds another player or against an offensive player whose hands are not tight against his chest when contact is made. "Roughness" and "unsportsmanlike conduct" cover any action that is a deliberate foul—such as jumping on a player who is already down, punching, tripping, kneeing, or elbowing—and may include cursing, arguing, or provoking a fight. More serious infractions can result in players' being expelled from the game. "Interference" penalties give the offense a completed pass and an automatic first down if any defensive man either keeps a receiver from catching a pass or makes contact with him while the ball is in the air. The receiver is not allowed to push the defender away either. And penalties are assessed if an ineligible receiver (interior lineman) leaves the line of scrimmage on a pass play before the ball is thrown, when a punter is hit after the kick, and when the passer intentionally grounds the ball.

—The whistle stops the play. A player should be taught that any time he hears a whistle, everythings stops. If he continues after the whistle he can be penalized.

—The offensive team has four plays to move the ball ten yards. Any time the ball is moved ten yards or more within those four plays the offense gets four more "downs." If they do not, they lose the ball to the other team.

—If a team moves the ball over the goal line it is a "touchdown," worth six points. After a touchdown the offensive team has one play to run, pass, or placekick for another point. In college a run or pass (play is run from the two yard line) results in two points, a kick one point.

Placekicking is usually too much for the early phases of youth-league play.

—If the offensive team moves the ball over the goal line without having possession, such as a pass that is intercepted or a fumble that rolls into the end zone and is recovered by the other team, it is a "touchback," worth zero points. The ball is put into play on the twenty yard line. If the offensive team brings the ball back over its own goal line and is stopped behind the line it is a "safety," worth two points for the other team. The offensive team then has one play to kick the ball away from its own twenty yard line. An interception by a defender that he then tries to run back from behind his goal line results in a safety if he does not make it out.

—A player with the ball who steps on or over any out-of-bounds line (sideline) is out of bounds and play is dead. A pass receiver must have both feet inbounds when he catches the ball, or else the pass is ruled incomplete.

The rules of the game are more complex than that, but the youngster who knows just that much will understand what he must to begin playing the game. Probably the most difficult difference he will have to master between practice and a game is the time constraint. It is one thing to be able to take all the time he wants to get ready for the play; it is something else to do it under the pressure of a clock. This is a team discipline that must be stressed and requires both on-the-field leadership by the kids themselves and training during practice. They must be taught to call "time-out" when there is too much confusion to continue. But they must also know that each team is limited to four time-outs each half and that only the captain can signal for time-out. Most important, they have to learn to be organized and discipline themselves to cooperate with the captain and quarterback.

They must also learn to get the "feel" of actually playing in a game, and the three most important variables they will find, are time, field position, and the relationship between down and yards to go for a first down. Working within these three variables the offense must learn to develop strategy and the defense counterstrategy.

The basis for offensive strategy is the play series. The offense is trying to run a play that the defense does not expect by careful use of play series and deception. Often a play is called by the quarterback not for its own value but to "set up" the play following. Traditionally such plays as a pass on third down, long yardage, and a power play or quarterback sneak on third down, short yardage, have come to be expected. The quarterback or the coach has to weigh what the team does best in making play-by-play decisions. And he does not have much time to do it. Another decision that the coach must make is—does he or the quarterback call the plays? If the coach calls the game from the bench he must have at least two players to shuttle in and out with the plays. Usually backs handle that assignment better at this level because they have broader understanding of the plays.

Defensive strategy is based primarily on trying to outguess the offense. While the quarterback is trying to decide what will work best, the defense is trying to guess what the quarterback will decide, yet knowing that they must be prepared for any eventuality. The defense should also be evaluating play sequences—to be able to see when the offense is trying to set up a certain play. Strategy is something that must be taught to beginners on both offense and defense. Concentrating on fundamentals, they often do not think beyond their individual positions. They have to constantly be challenged to consider the team, the game, and what everyone else is doing, without forgetting their own responsibilities. A comment concerning the play of a member of the other team to the coach or quarterback may result in calling just the right play. Maybe a linebacker always blitzes on third down or plays too close to the line, or a weak lineman is easily blocked out. The kids must be reminded over and over again to think as a team during practice so that it will come naturally during the game.

And if a young player is to successfully graduate into higher levels of play, there are two elements of the game he must learn. They are teamwork and good, solid fundamental play. If this book gets across that point and convinces coaches and parents of inexperienced players that they will achieve superior results by keeping things as simple as possible, it will have accomplished something worthwhile.

Youth leagues, under so much fire these days from critical parents, teachers, and psychologists, can be either exactly what the critics claim they are or one of the most highly contributory factors in a child's mid-years' positive development. The game should be fun, yet he should learn that to play it properly requires discipline, team effort, and hard work. He should learn that everyone makes mistakes, but success comes to the one who learns to correct them. He should learn to respect talent, desire, and dedication, and he should learn to keep giving his very best effort all the time. But he should not forget that he has a responsibility to his weaker teammate—to help him to learn to play better. Football is one of the finest vehicles we have to impress upon young people the need for those attributes which are so important in life and lead to respect and success later on. But the game must be used correctly.

A word about parents. More good football experience is destroyed by childish and immature parents and coaches than any other single element. Why cannot the onlookers let the kids play football without infusing all the negative effects of jealousy and bitterness that so dominate adult society? Why cannot parents see beyond their own little progeny and watch two teams play football?

Everyone involved with a youth league is generally inexperienced—the players, the coaches, and the officials. Yet the fans insist in blasting each with a humiliating degree of regularity. Some of the things parents shout to opposing players—eleven year olds—on a football field would embarrass a steel worker. A coach runs out on the field and screams at the referee until a mortified player tugs at his shirt and asks him to please leave the field. Another coach flies into a rage and tells his players to go out on the field and start punching the opposing players; the humiliated players quietly go out and play football. Parents yell at the coaches from the stands while loyal players burn with shame. If football is to teach sportsmanship, the youth league parents have the first lesson to learn.

The parent must also understand the goals and accept part of the responsibility to help the players to learn without unreasonable pressure and bad examples. If parents undermine the coach, they destroy the team. Yet if they ignore bad coaching they may be hurting their children. If other parents are turning the league into a free-for-all and you, as a parent, ignore it and let it happen, you stand the chance of your son learning to hate the game and becoming cynical. If you care and you understand the importance of the experience to your son and all the other sons, you and others like you can make the difference.

Coaches and parents must never forget that there is something much more important than winning a football game. That thirty-two, forty-eight, or sixty minutes on the field is a segment of your child's life and a piece of the growth of America's youth. If the adults foul it up with their own petty, selfish frustrations, they are contributing to all those things we detest that lead to juvenile delinquency and disrespect. And that is a heavy responsibility.

Index

126